Panel Quilting Mastery

A Comprehensive Guide to Creative Fabric Panel Projects

CAROLYN HOLT

Carolyn Holt

Table of Contents

Carolyn Holt

Book Introduction:

Panel quilting, although relatively modern in its popularity, offers both beginners and experts alike a chance to craft visually stunning quilts without the intensive labor of piece-by-piece creation. With pre-printed panels, the possibilities become nearly endless. Whether you're hoping to craft a sentimental gift for a loved one, a decorative masterpiece for your home, or even a commemorative piece that tells a story, this guide is your stepping stone.

Through the chapters of this comprehensive book, we'll guide you through the rich history of quilting and its evolutions. Delving deep into the tools and materials, you'll be equipped with the know-how to choose, maintain, and master each instrument. As you venture deeper, you'll uncover the secrets behind selecting panels that resonate with your vision and learn techniques to prepare, cut, and assemble them. By understanding the fundamental patterns and designs available, and even discovering advanced techniques, your quilted artwork will transcend from mere fabric and thread, into a piece of art.

Quilting is not just about assembling pieces. It's an art form, and like every art form, it allows for personal expression. From embellishments, which add sparkle, to troubleshooting techniques that ensure every project is flawless, we aim to empower you with knowledge and inspiration. With real-life projects, stories from fellow quilters, and a glimpse into the future trends of panel quilting, we hope this guide serves as more than just a manual - we hope it becomes your quilting companion.

Carolyn Holt

Quilting with panels opens up an exciting new world of possibilities for quilt makers. Panels featuring beautifully printed designs allow quilters to easily create stunning quilts, even for beginners. This comprehensive guide will teach you everything you need to know about quilting with panels. Discover how to make perfect quilting choices, plan your design, and incorporate panels into traditional and modern sewing techniques. With clear instructions, helpful tips, and inspiring photos, this book will give you the skills and confidence to master the art of panel quilting.

We'll start by exploring the wide array of printed quilt panels available, from traditional florals and geometric designs to modern motifs and whimsical themes. You'll learn how to evaluate quilt panel quality, scale, color palette, and more to choose the perfect panels for your project. Next, we'll cover planning and designing with panels using different layouts like medallion, borders, and blocks. You'll find out how to highlight focal panels or repeat multiple panels in pleasing layouts. Helpful guides show you how to balance the proportions of plain blocks, sashing, and printed panels.

The heart of the book features accessible step-by-step instructions for sewing gorgeous quilts with panels. You'll learn the basics of preparing and cutting panels for quilting, along with how to prevent distortion. Handy tips help you get perfect seam allowances when joining panels. Then, you'll move on to assembling your quilt using traditional piecing or timesaving shortcuts. Both machine and hand quilting techniques are covered, so you can finish your panel quilt to effectively and efficiently .

Advanced quilters will appreciate the information on designing custom panels and applying more complex techniques like applique, trapunto and embellishment, to take your panel quilting to the next level. You'll also find adaptations on how to use panels in trendy projects like bags, table runners, and home decor items for a modern handmade style. Full size quilting templates are included in a handy pocket.

Panel Quilting Mastery

With the techniques in this all-inclusive guide, you'll have the confidence to create spectacular quilts starting from printed panels. Both practical and artful at the same time, panel quilting opens up artistic possibilities from subtle tone-on-tone designs to eye-catching pops of color. Whether you're drawn to traditional, modern, whimsical or eclectic quilt styles, panel quilting has something for everyone. So, explore the creative possibilities and experience the joys of quilting with panels!

The beauty of this activity, in all its textured glory, lies not just in the final, tangible product. It also exists in the hours spent tracing patterns, selecting fabrics, and meditatively stitching each piece together. Quilting is as much a journey of passion as it is a practical craft. In the realm of this art form, panel quilting has emerged as a harmonious blend of tradition and innovation, offering fresh avenues of creativity to seasoned quilters and novices alike.

In The Comprehensive Guide to Quilting with Panels: Experience the Joy of Quilting and Create Stunning Artistic Projects, we embark on an exploration of this distinctive technique. This journey is not just about learning the skills, but also understanding the history, potential, and the heart of panel quilting.

The rise of panel quilting is a testament to the adaptive spirit of quilters. As time has progressed, with technologies bringing forth new materials and printing capabilities, the world of quilting was quick to embrace these changes. Panels allowed for intricate designs and detailed images to be pre-printed on fabric, saving time without sacrificing the complexity or aesthetics of a quilt. But, they were not just about convenience. Panels became a canvas for quilters to add their unique touch. This led to adaptation and innovation in the sewing industry.

From an outsider's point of view, , using panels may seem like a shortcut or a way to bypass the traditional quilting process. However, this could not be further from the truth. While panels do simplify certain aspects, they introduce their own set of challenges and opportunities. They invite the quilter to think differently, to strategize on complementing the panel's design, and to accentuate its beauty through quilting techniques.

Moreover, the world of panel quilting is vast. The variety of themes, from natural landscapes and wildlife, to intricate patterns or personal photographs, means that every quilter can find a panel that resonates with them. Panels serve as an inspiration. They are a starting point which each quilter can mold, adapt, and embellish according to their vision.

This book will not only introduce you to the practicalities of panel quilting like selecting panels, understanding the tools and materials, and mastering various techniques, but it will also immerse you in the stories and inspirations behind these creations. You'll meet quilters from around the world. Each has their own tale to tell and their own insights to share about this fascinating niche of quilting.

As we stitch together the narrative of panel quilting, we hope to inspire you to take up the needle and thread, to explore the myriad of possibilities that panels have to offer, and to create quilting masterpieces that will be cherished for generations to come. Whether you're a seasoned quilter looking to diversify your skills or a beginner eager to dive into the world of quilting, this guide promises a journey filled with learning, inspiration, and most importantly, joy.

Carolyn Holt

Chapter 1
Introduction to Quilting with Panels

Quilting is as ancient as civilization itself. Traces of this craft have been discovered in Egyptian tombs, Mongolian caves, and ancient European settlements. Originally born out of the necessity for warmth and protection, quilting quickly evolved into an art form. It became a canvas for expression and a testament to craftsmanship.

Panel quilting, while not as ancient, carries this torch forward. Initially, panels were used as centerpieces for quilts, often showcasing a scene or a stunning image, with traditional quilting methods surrounding this centerpiece. However, as the popularity of these panels grew, so did their applications.

What is it about panel quilting that has crafters, both new and experienced, so enamored? The allure can be attributed to a few key factors:

Efficiency and Speed: For many, the prospect of creating a quilt from scratch and piecing together numerous tiny patches, can be daunting. Panels provide a beautiful and intricate design without the countless hours of meticulous stitching.

A Canvas for Creativity: Panels, in their essence, are like blank canvases waiting for an artist's touch. With the base design in place, quilters can focus on enhancements through patterns, border designs, or embellishments.

Diversity in Design: From landscapes to portraits, from abstract art to detailed scenes, panels come in an astonishing array of designs. This plethora of options ensures that there's something for every quilter, regardless of their taste.

Panel Quilting Mastery

Skill Enhancement: Contrary to popular belief, working with panels isn't an 'easy way out'. It offers both novices and experts a unique set of challenges, allowing them to hone in on their skills.

Affordability: Crafting a quilt, especially one with intricate designs, can be an expensive endeavor. Panels, however, often offer an economical option without compromising on the visual appeal.

Quilting, in its essence, is a time-capsule of human innovation, creativity, and resilience. From its primordial forms in ancient civilizations, to the intricate, artistic masterpieces we see today, quilting has been a testament to human ingenuity. Within this vast tapestry of quilting history, panel quilting shines as a beacon of modern evolution, yet remains firmly rooted in tradition. Let's delve deeper into understanding its allure and significance.

A Historical Perspective

Long before panel quilting came into existence, our ancestors were stitching together layers of fabric to create warmth. The very act of quilting sewing two layers of cloth together with an insulating layer in between, was practical in nature. Ancient Egyptian sculptures show figures dressed in quilted wear, indicating that as early as 3400 B.C., quilting was an established craft. Fast-forward to medieval times, and we see knights wearing quilted garments beneath their armor for comfort.

But, when did the art of quilting transition from the purely functional to the decorative? Historical records from the 15th century onward, highlight a significant shift, with quilts beginning to feature artistic designs, motifs, and even narrative scenes. This period can be seen as a precursor to panel quilting, where the emphasis started to lean heavily on the aesthetic value and storytelling ability of quilts.

The 19th century ushered in a revolutionary era for quilting. With the Industrial Revolution came mass-produced textiles, making fabrics more accessible to the average person. Quilting bee communities emerged, where women would gather to quilt and share stories, strengthening both their quilts and social ties. It was in such a climate of innovation and community bonding that the seeds of panel quilting were likely sown.

Emergence and Rise of Panel Quilting

Carolyn Holt

The 20th century saw a rise in commercial printing techniques, which allowed for detailed images to be printed on fabric. Panel quilting essentially began as a byproduct of this technological advancement. Fabric manufacturers started producing panels as they realized the potential for quilters to utilize these as centerpieces or focal points for their quilts. These panels, with their vibrant colors and intricate designs, instantly appealed to quilters, both for their beauty and the convenience they offered.

Panel quilting, in its early days, was sometimes dismissed by purists as 'cheating'. After all, instead of painstakingly piecing together small bits of fabric to create an image, one could now simply buy a pre-printed panel. However, it soon became evident that working with panels required its own set of skills and creativity. The challenge shifted from creating a design to enhancing and complementing the pre-existing one.

Why Panel Quilting Resonates

Narrative Possibilities: A single panel can tell a story. Whether it's a serene landscape, a vivid wildlife scene, or a whimsical fairy tale portrayal, panels offer quilters a starting narrative, which they can then build upon and embellish.

Inclusive for All Levels: For beginners, a panel provides a sense of direction and alleviates the initial overwhelming feeling of starting from scratch. For seasoned quilters, it presents a challenge to enhance, highlight, and sometimes even transform the panel's narrative.

Time-Saver without Compromise: In today's fast-paced world, not everyone has the luxury of spending months on a single quilt. Panels offer a solution where quilters can still produce breathtaking works of art in a fraction of the time.

Diverse and Evolving: The range of panels available today is staggering. From abstract art to hyperrealistic images, every quilter can find panels that resonate with their aesthetic taste.

Panel Quilting Mastery

Quilting with panels opens up exciting new possibilities for both beginning quilters and experienced artists alike. Printed panel designs allow you to create complex-looking quilts in less time, even with little piecing experience. Meanwhile, incorporating panels in traditional quilt blocks or as focal points, gives advanced quilters the chance to add beautiful, intricate designs and work on perfecting their technique. This comprehensive guide will provide everything you need to successfully create stunning projects with printed quilt panels.

What Are Quilt Panels?

Quilt panels are pre-printed squares of fabric featuring complete quilt block designs, patterns, pictorial scenes, or other motifs. They come in standard quilt sizes from fat quarter up to king-size. Common panel designs include floral medallions, Americana motifs, geometric blocks, whimsical prints and much more. The designs are printed on high quality cotton fabric using pigment inks that resist fading and laundering. Premium panels may even use batik fabrics.

Panels provide quilters with a shortcut to adding elaborate looking designs without tedious piecing work. From a distance, multi-patch quilt blocks or intricate scenes on panels can mimic the look of complex quilting. Although up close, the continuous designs lack seams. Panels are a versatile substrate that can be cut up into blocks, framed by sashing, or quilted as is. They open up many options, from utilizing large scale focal points, to repeating all over patterns.

The Benefits of Quilting with Panels

Quilting with panels offers many advantages:

Shortcut to intricate designs with no piecing needed
Easily incorporate different themes and motifs
Provides focal points for medallion or block quilts
Allows beginners to make complex looking quilts
Faster and easier than piecing intricate blocks
Pre-printed panels reduce the fabric selection process
Panels come in convenient pre-cut sizes
Adds excitement and visual richness to quilts
Printed elements have seamless quality when quilted

Carolyn Holt

Complements pieced blocks in endless layouts
Guide to color palette and design planning
With pre-designed elements in place, you can focus on planning layouts, choosing coordinating fabrics, and perfecting your quilting technique when making panel quilts. Follow the steps in this guide, and even beginners can make stunning quilts with panels!

Types of Quilt Panels

There is an extensive range of panel designs available to accommodate both traditional and modern quilting tastes. Here are some of the most common styles:

Floral Medallions: Large floral motifs, rose bouquets, and flower medallions remain a quilting classic. Look for symmetrical designs with graceful curves and flourishes rendered in batik or muted tones.

Geometric Blocks: Updated prints featuring large-scale geometric designs from traditional blocks like Trip Around the World to Moroccan Tiles lend bold style.

Conversationals: Vintage-inspired conversational prints depicting charming vignettes, farmhouse scenes, and botanical drawings offer old-fashioned appeal.

Whimsical: From fairies and woodland creatures to dress forms and teapots, whimsical panels tickle the imagination and add playful personality.

Patterns: Updated takes on traditional quilt patterns like Lone Star, Grandmother's Flower Garden, and Double Wedding Ring adorn many modern panels.

Novelty: Prints featuring everything from skulls to steampunk gears bring funky, ironic flair.

Portraits: Stylized animal portraits, faces, and figures create focal panels and allow more artistic expression.

Panel Quilting Mastery

Text: Word prints containing inspirational quotes, dictionary pages, or cryptic text add conceptual intrigue.

Keep in mind that panels come in a range of sizes from fat quarter (18" x 22") up to king (108" x 108"). Smaller panels work well for block inserts or repeating patterns, while large, bold designs make striking focal points. Whether your taste runs traditional or modern, there are endless panel possibilities!

Incorporating Panels into Quilt Designs

Quilt panels provide the pre-printed design elements – the rest is up to your imagination! You have the freedom to cut panels into sections and combine them with pieced blocks in limitless layouts. Panels can be featured centrally as a focal medallion or inserted into block quilts for pops of style. Repeating all over printed panels or alternating them with solid sashing are other options. Skillfully stitching and finishing your panel quilt can be as important as the fabrics.

Quilting with panels allows you to develop your strengths as a quilter. For beginners, it provides a shortcut to stunning results while focusing on improving piecing technique and working with layouts. Intermediate quilters can showcase their quilting skills with elaborate custom designs. Advanced quilters can exercise creativity in using panels in non-traditional ways, like cutting and splicing them into original blocks. This guide will walk you through the entire panel quilting process step-by-step.

Chapter 1 Summary:

Quilt panels are pre-printed squares of fabric featuring intricate quilt block designs or pictorial motifs.

Panels offer shortcuts to complex looking quilts and focal design elements without piecing.

Benefits include easier design and color planning, convenience, and engaging visual style.

Many panel styles are available, from traditional florals and geometrics to modern themes.

Panels can be featured alone or incorporated with piecing in endless layout variations.

Carolyn Holt

Quilting with panels encourages technical skills and creative expression at any level.

Getting Started with Panel Quilting

One of the best things about panel quilting is that it's accessible to quilters of all skill levels. You don't need extensive piecing experience or mastery of complex blocks. Beginners can use panels as a shortcut to stunning results. Intermediate quilters can build skills incorporating panels into traditional quilts, and advanced quilters can exercise creativity in cutting apart panels or building intricate designs around them. With some preparation and planning, anyone can quilt beautiful projects featuring panels.

For your first panel quilt, start with some pre-planning. Browse through panel offerings online or in fabric stores until you find a design you love with colors that speak to you. Large scale floral medallions, geometric blocks, and conversational prints offer classic choices. For modern style, look for updated takes on traditional blocks or graphic art panels. See what inspiration strikes!

Unless you're happy with a simple two fabric quilt in the panel size, you'll need coordinating fabrics too. The panels themselves can act as a guide. Choose fabrics that pick up dominant colors from the panel print or provide pleasing contrast. Solid color fabrics are easy complements, but small prints and batiks also pair nicely with busy panels. Buy a bit more yardage than you think you'll need to give yourself design options.

Think about the quilt's purpose, too. Is it a baby quilt, wall hanging or bed sized decorative quilt? Your choices will influence decisions like scale and complexity. For most first panel quilts, a simple design like featuring the panel with plain sashing and cornerstones allows the print to shine. Don't overcomplicate it!

Once you have your fabric selections, wash and press everything before getting started. Then lay it all out and experiment with arrangement ideas. A design wall is ideal, but you can lay pieces on the floor or a bed too. See what pleases your eye. Snap some photos for review later, and don't on't stress about perfection. You can always tweak the layout when sewing.

Panel Quilting Mastery

Preparing Panels

With your fabrics and inspiration photos on hand, it's time to start preparing the quilt panels. Carefully read the manufacturer's instructions first. Prewashing and drying your panels is recommended to allow for any shrinkage and prevent distortion when piecing. Press panels gently on the back side with a warm iron to remove any folds or creases from packaging.

Inspect panels closely for any flaws in the fabric or printing. Tiny flecks are normal, but avoid panels with visible white lines, large spots, or misaligned designs. If you come across a panel you're not pleased with, return it for a panel with no imperfections. l. Check that designs are printed straight across the grain. Off-grain panels may skew when quilted. Measure panels precisely to ensure they are the labeled size. At times, you will find pre-cut panels may be off a bit.

Once prepped, it's safe to cut panels, if needed, for your design. Use an acrylic quilting ruler and rotary cutter for clean, straight cuts. Cut slowly and carefully to prevent dragging the fabric. Hold rulers firmly. Double check measurements twice before cutting irreplaceable panels! Save the remnants for smaller projects like bags or cushions.

Cutting panels into sections allows you to isolate design elements like a large flower spray or single block. Piece them creatively into medallion or block quilts along with your coordinating fabrics. For all over printed panels, you can simply trim to size in desired rectangle or square shape. Keep the orientation consistent when planning layouts.

Mark cutting guides with a washable marker, directly on panel fronts. To avoid ink bleeding, test markers first on a panel scrap. Mechanical chalk pencils are another option. Never use pins directly in printed panel fronts–they can leave permanent holes! Instead, use masking or painter's tape to make your cut lines. Remove tape immediately after cutting.

Piecing with Panels

Carolyn Holt

With panels cut to size, you're ready to start playing with layouts. Begin by auditioning arrangements of panels and fabric sections on your design floor or wall. Feel free to get creative and make changes as you go. No need to stick to initial plans if something else looks better! Just be cautious when handling cut panels to prevent stretching or distorting the edges.

Once you have a pleasing layout, be very careful when pinning to keep pins only in the seam allowances, never through the printed design. Use tape or clips if needed to avoid holes. Align and pin printed seams. Do the ends first.Thens do the edges. Pin perpendicular to the seam line, and usese plenty of pins for straight seams.

Practice stitching with scraps first. Use a medium length, straight stitch and high quality polyester or cotton thread that matches the panel color rather than contrasting. Test tension on scraps and adjust as needed to get smooth, even seams without puckers. Prepare to take it slowly. Remove any pins just before they reach the presser foot.

When joining panels, keep stitches in the seam allowance not on the printed design. Go slow and pivot at corners for sharp 90 degree angles. Keep panels flat and lined up as you sew, adjusting as needed. Avoid starting and stopping in the panel design area which can lead to backstitch holes. Sew off the edge of the panel instead.

Finger press seams flat before opening and ironing. Press gently from the wrong side using lots of steam and starch. Avoid ironing directly on panel print fronts as you can flatten and distort the designs. Let panel sections cool fully between pressing to prevent stretching.

With careful alignment, pinning, stitching, and pressing, panels will come together beautifully for a flawless quilt top ready for finishing! Just take it step by step. Correct any mistakes immediately by gently removing stitches rather than trying to reverse and resew. Have patience and keep panels flat andpinned securely. Continue with this practice until you achieve nice tight seams. Soon you'll have the confidence to piece intricate panel layouts!

Tips for Piecing Panels

Panel Quilting Mastery

Here are some top tips for success when cutting and sewing quilt panels:

Carefully read the manufacturer's instructions before washing and pressing.
Inspect panels closely and only use flawless quality prints.
Measure panels to ensure they are true to labeled size.
Mark cutting guides in washable marker, not pins.
Cut slowly with sharp blade to avoid shifting fabric
Pin and sew only in seam allowances, not through print design.
Use plenty of pins and finger press before opening seams.
Take it slowly! Machine stitch at moderate speed for control.
Pivot precisely at corners for sharp points with no gaps.
Remove pins just before they reach the needle to avoid snags,
Iron panels very gently through a pressing cloth on the wrong side.
Let panels fully cool between pressing to prevent stretching.
Handle panels carefully when joining to keep edges straight.
Make stitches smaller than usual(around 12 stitches per inch).
Be prepared to gently remove and re-sew if needed.
With some careful preparation, patience, and practice, you'll be ready to incorporate fabulous panels into your quilting projects. The results are well worth the extra effort! Still have questions? The next chapter will cover choosing the perfect panels in more detail.

Showcasing Panels in First Quilt Layouts

One of the joys of quilting with panels is seeing them transformed from printed fabric into stunning projects featuring your creative touches. For your first panel quilt, keep the layout simple to let the panels shine as the stars of the design. Focus on enhancing panels with coordinated fabrics and intentional finishing.

Single Panel Quilts

The easiest introductory layout features a single panel for a bold medallion style quilt. For bed and baby quilts, large scale panels around 50"– 60" work well. Smaller wall hanging panels can be used individually too. Surround a large central panel with multiple plain borders in coordinating fabrics and white sashing for definition. Standard borders finish at about 6" wide once sewn. Adjust to balance proportions.

For the center panels, florals, botanicals, and conversational prints make traditional options full of detail to practice quilting. Geometric and graphic panels offer bold negative space for heavy custom quilting. For any style panel, keep the fabric pairings simple. Contrast enhances both traditional and contemporary panels.

Once you have the central panel prepared, measure to calculate border and sashing dimensions. Cut side borders the exact vertical measurement of the panel and include seam allowances. Top and bottom borders will extend the full width plus allowances. Join borders with straight seams or simple 45 degree cornerstones. Add white sashing, then finish with the final borders.

The construction process will allow you to practice key techniques like achieving even borders, mitering corners, and getting perfectly square right angles on sashing. Go slowly, use ample pins, and press at each step. Check measurements twice. Don't be afraid to gently remove and redo any border or sashing strips if they don't align correctly. Keep making small adjustments to reachperfection.

Panel Inserts in Block Quilts

Another idea for an introductory panel layout is placing one or more printed panels into a basic block quilt design for pops of style. This allows you to surround panels in complimentary pieced blocks while developing fundamental piecing skills. For a cohesive look, choose a printed panel featuring the same block pattern or geometric shapes as the pieced blocks.

Play with different arrangements of alternating plain blocks and panel inserts on your design wall before sewing. You can substitute panels for blocks in a straight grid layout or scatter them across like picture frames. Try rotating panels or substituting half panel inserts into block rows. Don't be afraid to improvise until you find a pleasing arrangement.

Panel Quilting Mastery

When sewing, handle border blocks extra carefully during pinning, stitching, and pressing. Slow everything down further and use more pins to perfectly align joints between blocks and panels. Take time re-sewing, if needed, for seamless transitions with the printed designs. The extra effort results in stunning block quilts elevated by printed inserts.

Repeat Block Panel Quilts

Full panels featuring all over block prints allow you to quickly create bold, graphic quilts. Alternating or repeating quilt block panels with plain coordinating sashing strips, creates dynamic designs with dimension. Play with different width sashing and experiment mixing vertical, horizontal, and diagonal orientations.

Look for panels printed with tessellating block patterns that repeat seamlessly across the design like stars, hexagons, or interlocking geometric shapes. Scattered floral and conversation print panels can b
e fussy cut and positioned to create rhythmic repeats too. Printed strip panels are another option for fast pieced looks.

When preparing repeating panels, carefully align edges and endpoints where the print pattern meets to maintain continuity when piecing sashing strips between duplicated blocks. Precisely pin matching points before sewing. You can also improvise by intentionally spacing panels irregularly or across from each other, rather than leaving them aligned.

The graphic nature of repeating geometric and even floral panels brings exciting movement and energy to your design. Surround panels with low volume tonal solids or small scale prints to avoid competing visual distractions. The graphic panels should do the talking! Play up other bold choices like black sashing and bindings for modern edge.

No matter which simple layout you choose for your first panel quilt, the process will build essential skills from pressing to piecing to borders to finishing. Don't overwhelm yourself with numerous new techniques. Stick to the basics and handle panels gently. Supplementary videos or in-person lessons can help fill any knowledge gaps. Above all, have fun playing with beautiful panels as you continue your quilting journey!

Carolyn Holt

Next, we'll explore the abundant options you have to choose from and help you select winning panels for your quilting needs.

Chapter 2

Selecting the Perfect Panels for Your Quilt

Stepping into the world of quilting, especially panel quilting, is akin to entering an artist's studio. Just as a painter has brushes, palettes, and canvases, a quilter is armed with an array of tools and materials, each serving a unique purpose. Understanding these tools, their functions, and the materials at your disposal is fundamental in mastering the art of panel quilting. In this chapter, we will equip you with the knowledge to build your quilting arsenal.

Starting with the Basics:

Fabric Scissors and Rotary Cutters: These tools are your primary weapons in the quilting world. Fabric scissors should be sharp and reserved only for fabrics to maintain their edge. Rotary cutters, with their circular blades, allow for precise and quick fabric cutting, especially when paired with a quilting ruler.

Self-healing Cutting Mats: These mats, when used with rotary cutters, not only protect your workspace but also ensure accurate and clean cuts, thanks to the measured grid lines on their surface.

Quilting Rulers: These are not your ordinary rulers. They're designed specifically for quilting, they come in various sizes and shapes, and assist in measuring and cutting fabrics accurately.

Sewing Machine with a Walking Foot: While hand quilting has its charm, a sewing machine significantly speeds up the process. A walking foot ensures that the fabric layers don't shift while sewing, maintaining the quilt's integrity.

Selecting the Right Panel:

Panel Quilting Mastery

Just as a painter chooses a canvas size based on the envisioned painting, the selection of the right panel is crucial. Panels come in various sizes and materials. Here's what to keep in mind:

Material: Most panels are made of cotton, but you may also find options in silk, linen, or synthetic blends. Each material has its own texture and requires different care. Cotton is often the preferred choice due to its durability and ease of handling.

Size: Panels range from small, pillow-sized pieces to large, bedspread-sized ones. Your project's intent will dictate your panel size. For wall hangings, smaller panels might suffice, while quilts or bedspreads will require larger ones.

Print Quality: The clarity and color vibrancy are critical. Ensure that the panel's print is clear, with no smudging or color bleeding, as this forms the foundation of your quilt.

Understanding Threads and Needles:

No quilt is complete without the threads that bind it and the needles that weave the magic.

Threads: Opt for high-quality threads that don't fray or break easily. Cotton thread is commonly used for quilting due to its strength and natural feel. However, polyester threads, with their sheen, can add a decorative touch.

Needles: The choice of needle depends on your fabric. For cotton panels, sharp, medium-sized needles are ideal. If you're working with a thicker or more textured fabric, you might require a larger needle.

Additional Must-Haves:

Pins and Pincushions: Pins hold your fabric pieces in place before they're sewn together. Opt for sharp, rust-free pins.

Seam Ripper: Everyone makes mistakes, and a seam ripper is your eraser in the quilting world. It helps undo stitches without damaging the fabric.

Iron and Ironing Board: Pressing your fabric ensures it's free of wrinkles, making the quilting process smoother. Always iron your panel and other fabric pieces before beginning.

The increasing popularity of quilt panels has brought so many exciting options to choose from. Browsing the myriad of available prints and themes is one of the most enjoyable parts of planning a panel quilting project. With some guidance on what to look for in quality, style, and composition, you'll be equipped to select winning panels for your quilting needs.

This chapter will cover:

Where to shop for quilt panels
Evaluating panel quality and composition
Scale, proportion, and dimension considerations
Choosing traditional, modern, or novelty themes
Coordinating colors and visual interest
Working with panel repeats and formatting
Building a collection for flexibility
Follow these tips to pick panels you'll absolutely love, and transform them into stunning quilts!

Where to Find Quilt Panels

Quilt panels were once only found in limited selections at local quilt shops. Now a world of panel possibilities is available both in stores and online. Here are top sources to discover exciting new panel designs:

Local Quilt Shops: Support small businesses while seeing and feeling panels in person. Shops often carry exclusives.

Chain and Fabric Stores: Joann, Hancock, and major fabric retailers stock panels plus occasion exclusives.

Panel Quilting Mastery

Independent Designers: Browse unique panels from smaller, independent designers online or at shows.

Manufacturer Sites: Check out collections from major panel brands like Moda, In The Beginning Fabrics, and more.

Etsy: Find boutique designers, custom panels, and vintage panels in active, Etsy shops.

eBay: Search for discounted and out of print panels from past collections.

Online Shops: Retailers like Missouri Star Quilt Co. and Keepsake Quilting have huge online panel selections.

Don't limit yourself to just the panels presented in the shop or site search. Get creative with keyword searches using terms like "focal panel," "novelty print," "floral medallion" etc. You never know what you'll uncover.

Evaluating Panel Quality

All panels are not created equal when it comes to quality. Take time assessing panels closely before purchasing. Check that:

Fabrics are tightly woven, with no loose, open weaves which are prone to fraying.
Details are crisp and sharply printed with no blurring or pixelation.
Colors appear rich and saturated without dull muddy tones.
Selvages are cleanly finishe and front and back are neat & square.
Panel measurements match advertised size with no distortions.
Fabrics feel smooth, not overly stiff, with nice drape & hand.
Panel sits flat and does not curl or tent when laid out.
Designs align properly to fabric grainand are not crooked.
There are no flaws like print skips, streaks, stains, or needle holes.
Higher quality, 100% cotton, or batik panels justify their higher price for flawless reproduction, vibrant colors, and smooth feel. Avoid inferior panels with crooked fuzzy printing, distorted grain, blemishes, or creases. Panels are an investment; inspect them closely.

Carolyn Holt

Scale and Proportion Tips

Panels come in square and rectangular formats from 18" up to massive 60-108" panels fit for king quilts. Consider the project size and your layout plans when selecting panel dimensions.

For medallion quilts, choose an impressively scaled focal panel around 50-60". Smaller panels can get lost or look skimpy when surrounded by multiple borders. Scale up the border and sashing strips so the panel remains the visually dominant element.

When inserting panels into block quilts, opt for smaller 18-24" panels that mimic block size for balanced proportions. If the layout includes multiple panels, scale down to 12-15" for continuity.

All-over print panels must have enough pattern repeats to function in your planned orientation and layout. A 42" star print panel with 2 repeat blocks won't align horizontally across a 60" wide quilt.

Panels with multiple, irregular motifs like florals, allow fussy cutting to isolate and highlight elements. Larger patterns yield more cut options. Small designs look best left whole as inserts rather than cut.

Consider whether to trim panels to standard ruler friendly square or rectangle sizes or work with provided dimensions for more unique quilt shapes. Mind the grain and pattern flow when sizing panels down.

Traditional, Modern or Novelty Themes

Panels are available spanning every aesthetic from antique florals to pop culture themes. Choose panels that bring joy and fit your style.

For traditional quilts, seek out ornate floral medallions, scenic Americana vignettes, delicate tea botanicals, or reproductions of vintage quilt blocks. Stay within a cohesive color story for your quilt.

Modern minimalist quilts come to life with graphic panels in bold colors, solids, or prints. Geometric tessellations, large-scale abstract patterns, pixelations, and line art panels make focal points.

Panel Quilting Mastery

Whimsy and novelty prints add personality. Vintage animal sketches, fairy tale scenes, cheeky sayings, and pop culture icons become playful artistic statements.

Consider including special occasion or holiday panels to make homemade gifts more meaningful. Seasonal panels can be hoarded for use in future years, too. The options are limitless!

Coordinating Colors

Once you've identified promising panel prospects, look at color composition next. Inspect how colors are distributed across the panel. Do dark and light values provide good contrast? Are colors evenly dispersed or clustered in sections? How do colors relate to each other?

Panels with grouped blocks of color are super easy to coordinate with solids. Keep an eye out for value clashes between prints and background solids, though. Busy, multicolor patterns call for simple, low contrast solids to let the panels shine.

Monochromatic panels in analogous colors of a single hue are versatile. Pair them with neutrals, black and white prints, or introduce an accent color. Color dominance varies from panel to panel, so arrange potential partner fabrics and analyze color relationships.

For panels where colors look jumbled or difficult to match, convert images to grayscale. Seeing light and dark values simplified makes coordinating and balancing colors much easier. Don't overthink it, and you'll achieve color success.

Repeating Block Panels

All-over printed panels feature tessellating blocks that repeat in formation across the design. Study repeats and formatting to ensure panels will work for your planned layout and orientation.

The most versatile repeating panels feature blocks that align both horizontally and vertically, so the pattern is uninterrupted in either quilt orientation. Floral panels sometimes print patterns that only align properly in one direction, so think through formatting closely.

Look carefully at how motif edges meet, and consider the spacing between block repeats. Well-designed panels will have near seamless flow between repeats to mimic continuous quilting. Make sure the number of repeats will extend adequately across your intended quilt width or length.

Panels, with obvious disjointed gaps between block repeats or mismatched edges, will look choppy once sewn. Unless you plan to intentionally misalign repeating blocks, seek out panels with seamless pattern flows for best visual results.

Building a Panel Collection

As you find special panels that appeal to you, don't be afraid to purchase some for future quilting. It helps to curate a small collection of your favorite prints and palettes to pull from later when inspiration strikes. Just be sure to store panels properly.

Before washing, trimming or cutting into panels, press on medium heat with lots of steam to remove any creases from packaging and storage. Then refold with right sides together. Wrap panels loosely in acid free tissue or lightly seal in plastic to prevent dust settling into fibers.

Organize and store panel collections flat in drawers or bins to prevent creasing. You can file by color, story, theme, holidays, or seasons. Avoid direct sunlight, which can prematurely fade prints. Now, they'll be waiting whenever you're ready for your next panel quilting adventure!

With a little practice assessing options and zeroing in on quality, scale, and color, you'll become a panel pro. Trust your intuition in choosing special prints that speak to you. Discover your perfect panels and bring them to life in your quilting. Next up, we'll explore planning pleasing layouts and designs.

More Tips for Selecting Winning Panels

With the overwhelming selection of quilt panels now available, it helps to have a system when evaluating options to find your perfect matches. Keep these additional tips in mind as you assess panels for quality, scale, color, and design.

Panel Quilting Mastery

Test Fabric Quality

Don't just use your eyes when inspecting fabric quality and flaws. Rely on your sense of touch too, by gently rubbing the panel front and back between your fingers and on your cheek. High quality, 100% cotton, and batik panels will feel smooth, soft, and supple. The colors should appear richly saturated.

Lower grade panels often feel overly stiff and brittle. Blotchy printing lacks vibrancy under inspection. Tiny nubs on the surface likely indicate lower thread count fabric. If a panel feels rough or scratchy, keeps creasing when unfolded, or tends to curl up on the edges, leave it behind in search of superior quality.

Check Color Accuracy

The colors and values portrayed on your monitor may not accurately match the physical panel, depending on your screen calibration and lighting environment. When ordering online, look for panels sold by retailers who provide second angled views and close-ups of the prints rather than just tiny thumbnails.

If possible, find and order the manufacturer's coordinating solids or prints pictured with the panels to see the true colors together. When panels arrive, unfold and lay them out in natural daylight or lamp light to verify the colors suit your needs before proceeding with related fabric purchases. Retailers accept returns for any reason.

Read Label Details

Turn panels over and read fabric content, manufacturing information and washing guidance on the label to inform your decisions. Panels that are 100% cotton tend to fare better than polyester blends with fading and laundering. Though costlier, batik panels offer beauty, pop, and richness.

Panels printed overseas can be lower quality with less oversight, while independent designers, printing domestically in small batches, aim for exceptional reproduction quality. Follow any washing, drying, or pressing guidance carefully before cutting into panels to prevent distortion. All the instructions are important.

Mind Nap and Sheen

Run your hands across the panel surface to detect napping, the raised fibers that run a certain direction, similar to velvet or velour fabrics. Avoid heavily napped panels, which can cause sewing and quilting challenges. Light napping is often unavoidable with cotton, though. Just be sure prints align properly to the grain.

Similarly, inspect panel sheen under lighting. Does it appear matte and opaque or overly shiny and translucent? Sheer, gauzy, panels showcase quilting skills,t but can be troublesome for piecing intricacies. Play it safe with nicely balanced, mid-weight quilting cotton panels boasting subtle sheen.

Determine True Grain

Fabric grain can appear perfectly straight on panels while they're folded and packaged. But once washed, trimmed and unfolded grain may skew off perpendicular. This will cause panels to stretch and distort when worked into quilt layouts.

To find the true straight-of-grain, lightly spritz panels, then allow them to fully dry without tugging or shifting the fabric. Once dried, fold diagonally corner to corner. Then gently pull the opposite diagonal ends, noting any distortion. Straight grain fabric will pull evenly corner to corner, but off-grain panels will not.

Evaluate Backs of Panels

Most quilters focus on the beautiful fronts of panels while assessing options. But it's wise to also inspect the print consistency and quality on the reverse. Well constructed panels will appear nearly identical on the front and back.

Panel Quilting Mastery

Panels with loose, sloppy printing on the back, likely indicate poor quality control overall. If the design shows through to the back in a substantially distorted, blurry, or off-center way, it's best to leave those panels behind for ones with crisper definition on both front and back.

Audition Partner Fabrics

It's difficult to envision how colors and values will ultimately appear together once panels are surrounded by coordinating fabrics. As you assess panels, also pre-purchase small swatches of fabrics you are considering pairing such as 3 inch squares.

Lay the audition squares over and alongside panel sections to preview whether thecolor combinations achieve the contrast, cohesion, emphasis, and overall visual impact you desire.. Swatches help take the guesswork out of coordinating. Return anything that ends up clashing with, to the star panels.

Take Panels for a Test Drive

If permitted in your local fabric stores, request to remove panels temporarily from packaging to fully inspect them before purchasing. Sometimes flaws, creases or other issues don't appear until panels are opened and handled.

Ask to lay panels out, completely open, on a cutting table . Check alignment and color consistency in natural lighting. Look at the front and back and test the hand and drape. Never feel pressured to purchase a panel you believe to be flawed. . Any hesitation means it's not the right one.

Build a Swatch Book

Compile a notebook or binder with mounted fabric swatches of your favorite purchased panels for quick previewing later. You can note coordinating fabrics for   future project ideas. Add inspirational photos and sketches too. When seeking the perfect panel for a new quilt, just flip through your swatch book for ideas first.

Trusting your instincts, along with the knowledge shared here, will equip you to select winning panels to transform into showstopping quilts. Always evaluate quality, consistency, color, and scale first. Seek panels that make your spirit soar when you look at them. The joy will reflect in the quilting.

With your stash of wonderful panels ready, it's time to unlock the possibilities and start designing your custom quilts. Let's explore planning different layouts to showcase the panels you love.

Choosing Panels to Showcase Your Quilting Skills

For intermediate and advanced quilters using panels in projects, consider how certain prints and layouts will exhibit your quilting talents. Follow panel selection tips that play to your quilting strengths.

Pick Panels that Spotlight Superior Piecing

Intricate patchwork deserves equally complex panel counterparts. Busy conversationals, kaleidoscopic geometrics, and implied detail prints work well with detailed patching. . Make sure to contrast the order of precise seams against free flowing panel designs.

Panel inserts also test piecing precision when joining seamlessly with surrounding blocks. Attentive cutting, strict seam allowances, and perfect alignment make even subtle panel transitions shine. Choose designs with defined edges to beautifully transpose into patchwork.

Seek Panels that Flatter Your Quilting Style

Your quilting really emerges as the foreground artwork when panels provide minimalist negative space. Does your style shine with long flowing lines, geometric showpiece motifs, or tiny overall micro stippling? Let large graphic panels be your blank canvas.

Panel Quilting Mastery

Heirloom florals and soft watercolors offer wide open spaces for quilting to subtly emulate the style and energy in the prints themselves. You can choose similar motifs in thread painted detail,or go the modern minimal route with simple lines and shapes.

Pick Panels that Allow Embellishment Dazzle

Heavy embellishment demands lightweight panels to avoid overpowering the foundation fabric. Sheer backgrounds enable shadow work to show dimensionality. Metallic prints gain extra glow with crystalline, beading, and embroidery.

Text and sketch style novelty prints offer opportunities to highlight words and images with stitching. Try integrating dimensional flowers, buttons, and fabric manipulation on conversationals. Dense panels compete visually with embellishments, so go lightly..

Choose Panels to Contrast with Your Dominant Style

Challenge yourself by using panels that juxtapose differing aesthetics. Combine structured lines with amorphous watercolors, and watch new visual languages emerge from the design tension.

For radical contrast, take traditional prints into modern territory with bold sashing and unconventional layouts. Or, bring modern graphic panels to life within frameworks of classic blocks. Risk taking creativity can lead to original style.

Seek Out Special Panels to Inspire Art Quilts

For one-of-a-kind art pieces, discover painters' canvas panels and commissioned custom designs to integrate into mixed media works. Photographic panels provide a hyper, realistic effect.

Abstract art panels help break creative ruts with improvisational cutting and unconventional reconstruction. Meld, overlap, and fuse segments with other unorthodox materials for freedom from quilting norms. Make the panel the springboard, not the destination.

Let Panels Guide Nontraditional Color Choices

Become a color explorer by taking cues directly from unlikely hues embedded in panels. Chartreuse, coral, and teal floral patterns provide jumping off points for out-of-the-box palettes. Monochromes prompt wildly, imaginative partners.

Value is your friend for unifying disparate colors. Branch out from a shared gray reading, even when colors appear to clash at first glance. Cohesive contrast emerges from unlikely chromatic mixes, guided by the panel palette.

Consider Panels that Change With Light

Watch panels transform under varied lighting for a multidimensional effect. Iridescent prints shift subtly between pearl and bold depending on light and movement. Translucent panels, overlapping darks, reveal hidden aspects.

Backlit linen panels take on stained glass qualities. Panels with optical illusions distort perspective based on vantage point. Program lighting installations to move panels through artistic color phases.

With an expanded view of how panels can stretch your skills in new directions, approach selecting them with an eye for enhancing your strengths while expanding your horizons. Let panels capture untapped creative potential!

The key is choosing intentionally with purpose, not just whatever catches your eye. Determine what you want to accomplish in a project, then seek out panels to achieve it.

Specific Questions to Ask When Evaluating Panels

Finding your perfect panels involves much more than just choosing appealing designs. Asking the right questions during selection helps ensure panels have the qualities needed for your particular project vision and quilting skills.

Consider these specifics when assessing panels:

Panel Quilting Mastery

Does the quality appear high and consistent?

Inspect fabric, printing, color vibrancy and packaging closely.
Check for flaws in fabric or art reproduction.
Test hand and drape for softness and suppleness.
Are treatments like batik or linen suitable?
Is the scale and number of repeats adequate?

Measure dimensions precisely, don't just read labels.
Study repeat patterns to calculate layout compatibility.
Allow for trimming margins, kerfs, and seam allowances.
Will enlarged or reduced scales maintain design integrity?
Do I need to fussy cut or use panels whole?

Can key motifs be isolated within panel prints?
Do elements look complete when extracted from the whole?
Will cutting disturb seamless patterns or symmetry?
Are there enough panels to extract repeating elements?
Which quilting methods will panels show best?

Do solid panels offer blank slates for intricate quilting?
Will dense panels overpower light meandering filler quilting?
Is the texture too pronounced for trapunto or stuffing?
Will panels distort under dense stitching or embellishing?
Do colors and values coordinate pleasingly?

Assess hues and intensities under both daylight and lamplight.
Will lights and darks provide desired contrast?
What accent colors can I selectively pull from the palette?
Are there suitable neutrals to recede or grounds for enhancement?
Which partner fabrics will let the panels shine?

Do solids or subtle prints allow panels to dominate?
What styles and scale of coordinating prints make sense?
Should sashing match closely or offer bold contrast?
Will multiple panels compete or complement each other?
Does the theme or style inspire layout ideas?

Do traditional patterns suggest medallion or block layouts?
Can I fussy cut to create kaleidoscopic effects?

Will graphic panels pop within otherwise simple piecing?

Does a novel theme suggest borders that enhance the storytelling?

Trusting both your instincts and this thorough line of questioning, equips you to select spectacular panels purposefully matched to your quilt's design needs.Enjoy the journey of imagination and creation!

With your stash of panels selected and prepped, it's time to unlock their potential by planning inspiring quilt layouts. Let's explore options for showcasing the panels you love, in designs that match your personal style and skills. The fun of bringing panels to life awaits!

Chapter 3
Designing Your Quilt with Panels

A quilt is more than just a cozy blanket or a decorative wall piece. It is a story told through fabric. In panel quilting, the narrative often begins with the panel itself. Hence, the selection of the right panel and understanding how to design around it becomes the cornerstone of your quilting project. In this chapter, we delve into the process of choosing the perfect panel and transforming it into a quilting masterpiece.

Understanding the Role of Panels:

At its core, a panel in quilting is akin to a protagonist in a story. It is the central element around which other design elements revolve. Whether it's a serene woodland scene, a vibrant geometric pattern, or a nostalgic vintage print, the panel sets the tone and theme for the entire quilt.

Factors to Consider While Selecting Panels:

Purpose of the Quilt: Is the quilt meant to be a decorative wall hanging, a cozy blanket for winter nights, or a gift for a special occasion? The purpose will influence the panel choice. For instance, a children's quilt might benefit from panels featuring playful, whimsical designs.

Color Palette: Consider the primary and secondary colors of the panel. Will they complement the existing decor if it's for home use? Are they appealing to the person receiving the quilt? Understanding the color dynamics can make or break the final look.

Scale and Size: A large panel might be overwhelming on a smaller quilt, while a tiny panel might get lost in a vast quilt. Ensure the panel's size is proportionate to the overall quilt size.

Panel Quilting Mastery

Emotional Resonance: Quilting is an emotional journey. Select a panel that resonates with you or evokes the emotions you wish to convey through the quilt.

Designing Around the Panel:

Once you have your panel, it's time to design the rest of the quilt. Here's a step-by-step approach:

Choosing Complementary Fabrics: Drawing from the panel's color palette, select fabrics that either contrast or complement the panel. These fabrics can be solid colors, prints, or a combination of both.

Layout and Composition: Decide on the quilt's layout. Will the panel be the center with patterns radiating outward? Or, will it be placed off-center, with intricate designs leading to it? Sketching the design on paper can be immensely helpful.

Borders and Sashing: Consider adding borders around the panel to frame it or use sashing,thin strips of fabric, between the panel and other quilt blocks to provide separation and structure.

Quilting Patterns: Decide on the quilting patterns you'll employ. Will you stitch around the design elements in the panel (known as 'stitch in the ditch') or opt for free-motion quilting to add a layer of texture?

Embellishments: Think about any embellishments you'd like to add. Beads, sequins, or decorative stitches can elevate the quilt's aesthetics, especially if they complement the panel's theme.

Expert Tips:

Always Pre-wash Panels: Before starting the quilting process, wash the panel to prevent any future shrinkage or color bleed.

Test Stitch: Before quilting directly on the panel, test your stitch on a scrap piece to ensure the tension and design look right.

Carolyn Holt

Stay Flexible: While planning is essential, remain open to changes. As you progress, you might find certain design elements or fabrics not working as envisioned. Adapt and modify as needed.

You've selected gorgeous focal panels, coordinated luscious fabrics, and can't wait to transform them into a stunning quilt. Now comes the fun part - planning the layout to beautifully showcase your printed panels! With some guidance on composition and design basics, even beginners can create jaw-dropping quilts from printed panels.

This chapter will cover:

Design basics like balance, movement and emphasis
Classic layouts like medallion, blocks, sashing and picture frames
Planning layouts based on panel type and number
Using panels in repeating block formations
Achieving harmony with color and scale
When to follow established patterns
Tips for fussy cutting and asymmetry
Modern graphic options like pixelation
Negative space to make panels pop
Working with awkward panel sizes or shapes

Follow along to gain the knowledge you need to design your custom vision and   unleash your creativity with panels!

Quilt Design Basics

While panels provide pre-printed design elements, how you arrange and frame them impacts the overall composition and visual appeal. Begin by thinking about some basic principles of design as you plan layouts:

Balance – Place focal panels in position and scale them to feel visually balanced within surrounding blocks or sashing.

Movement – Use secondary panels, color flow and quilting lines to guide the eye across the quilt.

Emphasis – Make important elements, like printed panels, stand out with size, color contrast, intricacy, and placement.

Panel Quilting Mastery

Repetition – Repeat colors, blocks, panels, or motifs to create rhythm and reinforce themes.

Contrast – Combine panels with very different blocks, settings, and color values for interest.

Unity – Tie the layout together with color palette cohesion and complementary style.

Scale/Proportion – Design block and border dimensions proportional to panel sizes for balanced spacing.

Classic Quilt Layouts with Panels

Many quilt panel layouts draw from traditional approaches like medallion, block, and sashing formats. Panels lend themselves seamlessly to classic patterns but with more freedom and artistry.

Medallion Style

Medallion quilts feature a large central panel surrounded by multiple borders. Simple to execute, this style provides great impact, showcasing focal panels. The central panel can be printed or pieced for contrast. Add gradually smaller borders, working out from the center.

Block Quilts

For block quilts, substitute printed panel units for some blocks within straight set formations or scattered layouts. Panel inserts add dynamism and intricacy against pieced blocks. Surround panels with coordinating fabric blocks, or alternate print and solid blocks.

Sashing Layouts

Sashing provides structure and definition when joining blocks or panels. Use colored sashing between the same panels to create rhythmic repetition. Swap vertical and horizontal orientations. Frame panels individually in sashing "picture frames."

Planning Layouts by Panel Type

Certain panel types lend themselves to particular traditional or original layouts.

Floral Medallions – These are perfect for centralized medallion quilts. Size them appropriately, according to quilt dimensions. Surround the panel with cut contrast blocks or pieced borders.

Conversationals – Scatter vignette panels across a block quilt to tell a story. Leave negative space around each one.

Large Scale Geometric Blocks – Create striking interlocking tessellations by repeating multiple patterns. These are effective in representing a modern, minimalist style.

Novelty Panels – Let whimsical panels shine as lightly framed focal points against plain quilted backgrounds.

All Over Toss Prints – Align repeats horizontally, vertically, or diagonally for fast kaleidoscope effects, and add short sashing between.

Playing with Panel Repeats

All over panel designs, featuring tessellating blocks, provide dynamic options for layouts. Repeat identical panels to form a patchwork quilt top with little piecing needed. Another idea is to play with creative alignments:

Align blocks horizontally, vertically or diagonally
Rotate alternating blocks for variation
Overlap opposing blocks slightly to interlock
Slice repeating blocks apart, then rearrange
Insert contrasting blocks or sashing between repeats
Leave negative space between grouped blocks

Panel Quilting Mastery

The rhythm created by repeating blocks brings great energy and movement to panel quilt layouts. Take advantage of those tessellating properties!

Achieving Harmony and Unity

A cohesive quilt starts with a balanced use of colors, scales, styles, and visual weight. Keep prints and blocks in similar scale for consistency. Work through these steps:

Determine color palette – Force hues into a color family by changing images to black and white and looking for value balance.

Audition fabric scales – Arrange prints by size gradient to create a cohesive scale.

Assess visual weight – Heavy, intense panels need airy space around them. Remember, bold prints pair with solids well.

Check for harmony – Do colors and fabrics complement but offer enough contrast?

Evaluate movement – Does the eye flow across the quilt through color, arrangement, and themes?

Consider formats appropriately – Save large panels for centralized focus, and scatter small vignettes across blocks.

Unify settings – Match sashing and cornerstone colors with prints for cohesion.

By honoring design fundamentals as you arrange panels and supporting fabrics, even contrasting layouts will feel unified thanks to balanced color, scale, proportion, value, and movement.

When to Follow Established Patterns

For beginners, use published patterns made specifically for working with panels, to learn successful layouts and structure before branching out. Pattern companies, like Panel Plates, offer tons of options.

Verify details:

Suitable panel size and number needed
Yardage requirements for borders and blocks
Block dimensions and number
Finished vs unfinished measurements

Carolyn Holt

Cutting instructions for panels and fabrics
Assembly order and diagrams
Quilting recommendations
Follow patterns precisely your first few times before modifying layouts or improvising   on your own. Learning what works through patterns gives you a larger knowledge base..

Tips for Asymmetry and Fussy Cutting

Non-traditional layouts like asymmetry and fussy cutting panels create energy and modern appeal.

Try fussy cutting small portions of panels to isolate motifs, like large flowers or single blocks, rather than using panels as a whole. Arrange cut sections to create new patterns when pieced.

Avoid symmetry and perfect repeat by intentionally shifting or rotating blocks and panels for a collage style layout. Overlap elements and vary block placement.

Cut panels into intriguing shapes like circles, diamonds, or triangles rather than just squares and rectangles. Angle edges for dynamic lines. Mix black and white with brilliant colors.

Feel empowered to find your own perfect layouts and quilting vision. But until you build experience, leverage patterns as guides, so you don't overlook key planning elements.

Modern Graphic Layouts

The strong lines and geometric shapes of many printed quilt panels lend themselves beautifully to modern minimalist layouts. Take advantage of graphic panels with these tips:

Pixelate – Enlarge motifs from panels or slice them into block units to scatter in grid or zigzag formations across solid backgrounds.

Negative Space – Isolate graphic portions of panels then surround them with wide negative space to create floating effects.

Panel Quilting Mastery

Color Pop - Choose panels with a strong color story like black & white graphic prints and make them pop against solid black backgrounds.

Sliver Panels — Slice elongated panels into narrow vertical or horizontal slivers and insert between solids like tunnels.

Modern Blocks — Replace some traditional blocks in patterns with graphic panel prints for contemporary edge.

Improv - Cut multiple identical panels into abstract shapes and improvise piecing them back together in new ways.

Line them up — Use linear panels as bold horizontal or vertical columns running the length or width of quilts.

Follow your intuition for free form compositions or structured layouts. Graphic panels empower modern quilting.

Embracing Negative Space

Whether going boldly modern or keeping it traditional, generously embracing negative space makes printed elements shine.

For medallion layouts, size borders appropriately so the dense, central panel still dominates. Too many competing patches of fabric diminish the impact.

Surround isolated panel vignettes with sizable frames of negative space rather than crowding multiple elements together. Let the eye travel across negative space to land on each print.

When fussy cutting panels into individual design elements, resist crowding them back together like a puzzle. Float each piece in its own space for proper appreciation.

Negative space allows the eye to rest and refocus between printed details. Don't fear large voids; balance panels thoughtfully with breathing room.

Working with Awkward Panel Shapes

Panels come in all sizes, including non-standard dimensions that require creative layout solutions.

Extra Wide Panels – Slice continuous designs, like scenics, into multiple sections to be scattered across quilts. Add sashing and cornerstones.

Extra Long Panels – Maintain impact by keeping elongated panels whole as a horizontal focal strip. Flank with compatible vertical blocks for increased interest.

Small Scale – For tiny panels, create a cluster of framed mini vignettes. Mix them with solid blocks rather than forcing a full layout.

Narrow Panels – Stack or alternate vertical sashing and narrow panels for an artsy modern result. Vary width and colors.

Odd Shapes - Highlight shaped panels, like circles and hexagons, by placing them within framed negative space or alternating them with shaped blocks.

With thought and care, any panel can be the starting point for inspiration. Let the elements you have on hand guide you toward creativity, not restrict it.

By learning and applying fundamental design principles as you plan your custom layouts, even beginners can achieve beautiful, balanced quilts from printed panels. Put these tips into action and create your quilt vision!

More Quilt Design Tips and Layout Inspiration

Take your quilt layout skills to the next level by digging deeper into design considerations and seeking unconventional inspirations. Keep these additional tips in mind as you envision transforming your treasured panels into quilts:

Panel Quilting Mastery

Think Beyond Borders

While simple borders nicely frame panels, don't be afraid to break out of the border box. Extend panels or design elements into asymmetric edges, or overlap panels over block edges for dimension. Let panels guide improvised piecing and angled seams.

Consider Scale and Balance

Enlarging or reducing the scale of panels and blocks from their original dimensions, changes visual weight and balance. Oversized panels become bold focal points, and miniaturized elements recede. Play with relative sizes to direct emphasis.

Focus on Consistent Quality

Quilt appeal relies on consistent quality across all components. Low grade fabrics and rough piecing diminish overall polish. Surround prized panels only with equally meticulous workmanship to maintain their luster.

Improvise with Panels

Look for opportunities to highlight panels in improvisational ways. Slice specialty shapes to scatter at random angles, or overlay transparent panels on background fabrics for layered dimension. Drape panels over molded forms for organic shapes.

Find Inspiration in Art Movements

Different art styles provide tons of inspiration for creative layouts:

Op Art - Use contrasting graphic panels to create optical illusions.
Cubism - Rearrange panel slices abstractly to show multifaceted perspective.
Minimalism - Isolate single bold panels against vast negative space.
Conceptualism – Juxtapose word panels purposefully to convey meaning.
Pop Art – Incorporate novelty panels with psychedelic colors and hip culture icons.

Reimagine Panels Unconventionally

Think beyond using panels as intact squares or rectangles. Slice into Polaroid-like frames, zig zag one panel into a full quilt top, or appliqué specific motifs onto fabric backgrounds. Repurpose panels for bags, clothing, or jewelry. There are no creative limits!

Reflect Your Inspiration

Let the quilt design mirror the prominent panel motif or style. Botanical prints inspired by nature complement organic, flowing lines. Geometric panels come to life within rigid structure and order. Your inspiration is the map. Follow it intuitively.

Leverage Value for Impact

Monochromatic, or similarly hued panels, sing when surrounded by fabrics of clearly contrasting values. Squint your eyes to see panels and fabric as only lights and darks. Use value contrast to make focal panels prominently pop.

With an expanded perspective on possibilities, view panels as the launch point to guide your wildest vision. Remember, if you don't love the result, you can always redo layouts until you achieve perfection. Follow your creative bliss!

Next we'll explore key techniques for preparing panels by prewashing, pressing, straightening the grain, and removing distortion.

Advanced Tips for Elevating Panel Quilt Designs

Take your panel quilt design skills up a notch with these advanced tips and unconventional approaches:

Utilize Illusory Depth

Panel Quilting Mastery

Layer sheer panels over darker substrates to add illusory depth. The transparency reveals partial hidden elements, like a fog. Stack multiple sheer layers for added dimension. Illuminate panels from behind for stained glass effects.

Incorporate Dimensionality

Physically build up dimension on otherwise flat panels by overlapping appliquéd shapes, beading, crystals, ribbons, buttons, and charms. Trapunto embroidered designs beneath panels or heavily quilt around shapes. Sculpting panels over molds adds visual appeal too.

Play with Perspective

Fussy cut panels into dynamic angles, corners, and road-like vanishing points to convey perspective on two-dimensional planes. Work to visually fill in perceived depth and add shadows.

Take a Painterly Approach

Soften hard panel edges by distressing, overdyeing, and tea staining raw panels before fussy cutting motifs. Overprint transparent sheer panels with thickened dye. Sketch or hand paint to meld with printed elements.

Make Unexpected Color Choices

Jump outside your comfort zone by choosing unexpected hues in panels. Pair magenta florals with lime green. Surround turquoise blocks in orange. Boost contrasts and reimagine palettes.

Let Panels Dictate Next Steps

Rather than entering projects with fixed outcomes planned, let the nature of each unique panel organically guide the techniques used to best showcase and enhance it. Follow their prompts and see where it takes you. .

Carolyn Holt

Lean into Counterintuition

Break the "rules" of conventional quilt planning to create intrigue. Pair large panels with tiny pieces to generate contrast. . Tightly crop around central motifs. Amplify imbalance and intentionally skew alignment.

Make Bold Graphic Statements

Use strong linear panels or sparse graphic prints to make bold, monochromatic statements when paired with wide, negative space and narrow framing. Scale up motifs into patterns.

Find Harmony in Chaos

Embrace the chaos! Busy art panels suggest rich free-form, dense piecing. Scatter motifs across manic kaleidoscopic arrays, and be reassured that complexity balances chaos.

Start with Meaning

Begin projects conceptually with panels that convey meaning or significance. Plan supporting fabrics and make quilting choices that symbolize and   reinforce the underlying message or honor the inspiration.

With an expanded perspective, view panels as your collaborator in the artistic process. Let their nature guide you toward creativity and meaning, not arbitrary plans. See where the panel wants to take you!

Chapter 4
Preparing Panels for Quilting

While the panel serves as the quilt's centerpiece, it is often the additional techniques, intricate detailing, and creative touches that elevate a quilt from a fabric assembly, to a work of art. This chapter explains various techniques and tricks that can enhance and complement your panel quilts, turning them into masterpieces.

Highlighting with Thread work:

Stitch in the Ditch: This is a technique where you sew right into the seam, or the "ditch", between two pieces of fabric. For panel quilts, this can be a way to highlight certain features of the panel without overtaking its inherent design.

Free-Motion Quilting: A method where the quilter moves the fabric freely under the needle to create decorative patterns, from swirls and loops to more intricate motifs. This technique can be used to add texture and depth around, or even on, the panel.

Appliqué to Add Dimension:

Appliqué involves taking a fabric shape and sewing it onto a larger fabric base. For panel quilts:

Overlay Appliqué: Add additional fabric shapes onto the panel to create a 3D effect or to emphasize certain elements.

Shadow Appliqué: Place a sheer fabric over the panel and stitch around shapes or motifs, creating a shadow effect. This can add depth and intrigue to the panel.

Panel Quilting Mastery

Borders and Frames:

Using different borders can dramatically alter the appearance of the panel quilt:

Multiple Borders: Layering several thin borders around a panel can create a framed effect, drawing attention to the panel.

Pieced Borders: Instead of using a solid strip of fabric, piece together different fabrics to create a border, introducing additional colors and patterns.

Using Embellishments:

Beads and Sequins: Sewing these onto the panel, or around it, can add sparkle and catch the eye. This works especially well for panels that depict night scenes or festive themes.

Ribbon and Lace: Introducing these elements can provide a touch of elegance and softness to the quilt.

Fabric Painting and Dyeing:

Enhancing Panels: If you feel that your panel lacks a certain color or intensity, carefully use fabric paints to add highlights, shadows, or other details.

Tie-Dye Effects: For the surrounding fabric, consider tie-dyeing techniques to introduce a burst of colors that complement the panel.

Expert Tips:

Practice on Scraps: Before applying a new technique directly onto the quilt, always test it on scrap fabric first.
Balancing Act: While it's tempting to use multiple techniques, ensure they harmonize with the panel and not overpower it.

Quality Over Quantity: Instead of numerous embellishments, sometimes a single, well-placed bead or a touch of fabric paint can make all the difference.

Playing with Texture:

The texture in a quilt can add depth, intrigue, and tactile appeal. Here are ways to play with texture in panel quilting:

Trapunto: An Italian-origin technique where certain areas of the quilt are stuffed, producing a raised surface. When strategically used in panel quilting, trapunto can highlight specific elements of the panel, making them pop.

Ruching: This involves gathering fabric in a repeating pattern to create ruffles or scallops. Introducing ruched fabric around a panel can provide a soft, cloud-like border, ideal for dreamy or romantic panels.

Raw Edge Appliqué: Instead of the traditional turned-edge appliqué, leave the edges of your appliqué fabric raw. With time and washing, these edges will slightly fray, giving a rustic and textured appeal.

Incorporating Modern Techniques:

Digital Printing: If you can't find the perfect panel, why not create one? Digital fabric printing allows you to use personal photos or designs, converting them into unique quilt panels.

Laser Cutting: For precision in intricate shapes and designs, especially for appliqué, laser cutting can be a valuable technique. It ensures clean cuts, saving time and reducing errors.

Mixing Fabric Types:

Incorporating different fabric types can bring about a variety in texture and appearance:

Velvet and Silk: Introduce patches or borders of these luxurious fabrics to add sheen and softness, contrasting the cotton panel.

Panel Quilting Mastery

Denim or Burlap: For a rustic or contemporary quilt, mixing rugged fabrics can bring about a unique charm.

Quilt As You Go (QAYG):

While traditionally, quilts are pieced together and then quilted, the QAYG method involves quilting individual sections and then joining them. For panel quilts:

Sectional Highlighting: Quilt individual sections around the panel differently, emphasizing various parts. When joined, it creates a mosaic of quilted patterns.

Ease and Manageability: QAYG makes managing large quilts easier, especially for beginners. It allows for focused attention on smaller sections, ensuring precision.

Binding Innovations:

Binding is the fabric that covers the raw edges of the quilt. While it's primarily functional, creative bindings can also be decorative:

Flange Binding: This introduces a thin strip of accent fabric between the quilt and the main binding, offering a piped effect.

Reversible Binding: Using a contrasting fabric for the binding means the quilt can be flipped and used on either side, giving a fresh look.

Expert Tips:

Stay Updated: The world of quilting is dynamic. New techniques and tools emerge regularly, so stay connected with quilting communities online or join a local quilting club to stay updated.

Document Your Process: Keeping a journal of the techniques you've tried, samples of stitches or fabrics, and notes on what worked or didn't, can be an invaluable resource for future projects.

Trust Your Instincts: While techniques and guidelines are helpful, your instinct and vision for the quilt are paramount. Don't be afraid to experiment or diverge from the conventional path.

You've selected gorgeous panels and planned inspiring layouts to showcase them. Now it's time to get your panels prepared by prewashing, pressing, straightening, and removing distortion and flaws. Proper preparation prevents problems down the road! Follow these steps:

Prewashing Panels

Prewashing panels before cutting them for quilting is highly recommended to prevent shrinkage and bleeding later. Wash in mild detergent on a gentle cycle. Don't overload washers and air dry to prevent heat damage.

Check first if panels have special washing instructions. Some need to be professionally "wet" cleaned. Inspect after washing to ensure dyes didn't run or fade. Press dry panels well with light steam.

Straightening Grain

Panel grain can shift off the straight of grain during manufacturing. This causes distortion when cut. Check grain by gently tugging diagonally from corner to corner. Fabric should hang straight with no pull. If needed, lightly spritz panels and press again to straighten grain.

Removing Fold Creases

Panels often retain creases from tight folding. Gently press with steam on the wrong side to remove creases embedded in the fibers before they become permanent. Avoid excess pressure, which can warp delicate fabric.

Inspecting for Flaws

Examine panels closely front and back for any flaws which will transfer to the quilt. Look for:

Panel Quilting Mastery

Printing inconsistencies, like white lines or blurring
Misaligned designs or crooked print across grain
Holes, runs, stains, dye spots, or bleed through
Adhesive or pin residue marks that have damaged fabric
Abandon flawed panels. Holes and stains will only enlarge when quilted.

Cutting Away Selvage Edges

Factory edge selvage contains extra sizing, dyes, and finishes that can cause fabric puckering. Trim away selvage edges before cutting for quilting. This prevents distortion along panel outer edges.

-

Removing Distortion

To prevent stretched out corners or edges, refold panels exactly on grainlines which are pre-pressed into the fabric. Refold hemming under any longer edges. Use spray starch and iron at a very low temperature as needed, to press flat without risking glues on the fabric.

Take steps during quilting to avoid introducing distortion through pulling on bias grain edges or inadequate pinning. Handling panels gently prevents stretching, prior to final quilting stitches, locking them into shape.

With perfectly flat, straight, and undistorted panels ready for cutting and piecing, you can proceed confidently knowing your panels are prepped for quilting success. Next, we'll discuss cutting techniques and layout considerations to maintain integrity when incorporating panels into your stunning quilts.

Additional Preparation Tips for Flawless Quilt Panels

Achieving pristine quilt panels requires going beyond just quick pressing and washing. Follow these additional steps to meticulously prep panels and ensure they are flawless:

Carolyn Holt

Test Fabric Density

Examining fabric density and thread count helps avoid problems. Hold panels up to the light and look for loose open weaves prone to fraying and seam issues. Dense, smooth fabrics withstand stress. Test density by gently rubbing and tugging panel corners.

Verify Straight Edges

Selvages and edges may appear straight while folded. Once washed and pressed, gently tear strips from both selvages. Trim one end straight then align selvage edge to trimmed end. If edges match precisely, the grain is square.

Check for Bowing

Press washed panels, then lay singly, on a flat surface. Smooth gently from center toward corners. If edges lift rather than lie flat, the panel has a slight bow from tension in the grain, which can worsen when pieced.

Watch for Skewing

Align pressed panels on top of an identical panel print. If motifs or grainlines don't match precisely, the bottom panel has skewed off grain. This causes distortion when aligning repeating prints.

Test Seam Allowance Space

If you're planning for partial seam allowances, test to make sure margins around the panel design allow adequate space for trimming, sewing, quilting, and binding. Measure precisely before cutting to verify workable space.

Consider Panel Backings

Panel Quilting Mastery

For translucent panels, inspect backing fabric. Its quality will impact quilting. Low thread counts create show-through shadows , and opacity prevents shadow details. Test layers together before committing.

Assess Panel Shape

Panel edges should align precisely with the straight of grain. Test by measuring each direction to check for rectangular shape. Trim to straighten "off-kilter" edges. Handle gently to avoid stretching bias sides.

Check Shrinkage Ratios

Prefabricated panels may have specialized finishes that alter shrinkage rates compared to yardage. Compensate by prewashing all fabrics multiple times separately and air drying fully to match shrinkage.

With deliberate attention to metrics like density, alignment, and shape, you can identify and resolve any panel flaws or inferior quality before investing significant effort into quilting. Strive for perfection in your panel prep to ensure success!

Precise Steps for Prewash and Pressing Perfection

To achieve pristine, dimensionally accurate quilt panels ready for flawless construction, follow these precise steps for prewashing and pressing:

Prewashing -

Check labels for any special washing instructions and fiber content.
Wash panels separately from other fabrics to prevent dye transfer.
Use a mesh bag for delicate fabrics to avoid pulling or snagging.
Wash in cold water on the gentle/delicate cycle with a mild detergent.
Rinse thoroughly in cold water to remove all soap residue.
Air dry panels flat, never machine dry to prevent heat damage.
Repeat washing if water remains cloudy to fully clear dyes and chemicals.
Steam press washed panels well before cutting to remove any creases.

Pressing -

Press panels one at a time on a wool pressing mat to prevent impressions.

Use a high steam iron on the cotton/linen setting to hydrate fibers.

Hold iron just above the surface and wait for steam to penetrate; avoid direct contact.

Gently smooth the entire panel surface, working outward from the center.

Flip panels over and iron the backside to relax fibers.

Check grain lines by tugging diagonally in both directions - fabric should hang straight.

If needed, lightly spritz skewed sections and repeat pressing until the grain is straightened.

Allow panels to fully cool and dry between pressing to prevent distortion from residual heat.

Refold along grain lines, pressing over the creases; store flat until ready to cut.

With careful prep and pressing, your panels will be perfectly ready for chopping, piecing, embellishing, and so much more! Follow these steps to start off every panel project right.

Preventing and Correcting Distortion in Quilt Panels

No matter how carefully handled, some distortion may still occur when working with delicate printed quilt panels. Watch for and mitigate these common causes of distortion:

Grain Skewing - Improper grain causes the greatest distortions when piecing. Periodically check grain lines and straighten as needed with spritzing and pressing.

Improper Folding - Refold panels precisely on grain crease lines. Improper folds lead to permanent skewing.

Inadequate Pinning - Insufficient pins allow fabric to shift and stretch when handling. Profuse pinning maintains alignment.

Insufficient Seam Allowance - Skimpy margins get consumed during construction stages. Plan for 1/4" finished allowance minimum.

Panel Quilting Mastery

Inappropriate Marking - Mark quilt tops, not panel fronts. Test markers first for bleed potential before using.

Pulling on Bias - Gently handle edges to avoid tugging the bias grain and causing stretch.

Hasty Seam Rippling - Ripping out errors can distort fabric along rip lines. Gently steam, press flat.

Excessive Heat - High iron heat can shrink or melt fabrics. Use appropriate temperature for fiber content.

Overhandling - Repeated folding, creasing and handling can fatigue fabrics. Handle panels as little as possible.

Improper Pressing - Direct iron contact and excess pressure can crush fabric texture. Press delicately.

To correct distortions, fully wet down problem areas, gently work fibers straight, pin in place tautly, and press dry. Check results under raking light and repeat until each panel lies perfectly flat and undistorted.

With caution and preventative steps, you can achieve flawlessly flat panels ready for intricate piecing and quilting. Gentle handling preserves their pristine condition. Next, we'll explore cutting techniques to maintain panel integrity when incorporating into quilts.

Advanced Preparation Techniques for Flawless Panel Integration

Moving beyond basic washing and pressing, advanced panel preparation techniques ensure flawless integration into intricate quilt layouts.

Testing Panel Dimensions

Don't assume panels meet exact size specifications. Subtle distortions during manufacturing can result in panels being slightly off. Precisely measure and mark borders and block dimensions directly on each panel before cutting to compensate for any deviations.

Carolyn Holt

Verifying Print Alignment

On repeating block prints, compare alignment marks across panels to make sure the pattern matches precisely. Even slight print misalignments become obvious once panels are pieced together.

Squaring Off Edges

Use an acrylic ruler and rotary cutter to square off uneven edges on rectangle panels, so all borders are 90 degree angles. Avoid skewed edges throwing off quilt layouts.

Refining Large Prints

For panels with text or large prints, trim away excess borders, so motifs are framed within the block, rather than spanning into seam allowances. This prevents dissecting words or images when piecing.

Accounting for Seam Allowance

If your planned layout depends on precise, partial seam allowances, measure and mark margins from printed motifs before cutting to ensure adequate space remains for stitching.

Pre-Shrinking All Elements

Since most panels have a finish, shrinkage rates may vary. Prewash and press all panels, fabrics, and threads to fuse projects under equivalent pre-shrinking, preventing later distortion.

Pressing Panel Backs

Avoid skipping panel backsides when pressing! They need equal moisture and heat to relax fibers and stabilize grain alignment. Press fronts and backs before precision cutting.

Panel Quilting Mastery

With scrupulous preparation, you can cut panels knowing all elements are squared, aligned, matched in shrinkage, and ready for your most intricate layouts. Proper panel prep removes doubt about distortion, so you can piece confidently.

Carolyn Holt

Chapter 5

Sewing Panels into Quilt Tops

Every quilting project is a dance of fabric and color. The choices you make in this realm can either elevate your panel quilting to the realm of artistry, or leave it lacking in cohesion and visual appeal. This chapter delves deep into the world of fabric selection and color theory, arming you with the knowledge to make informed decisions that harmonize with your chosen panels.

Understanding Fabric Types:

While cotton is a staple in quilting, there are several fabric types to consider:

Cotton: Breathable, durable, and easy to work with, cotton is the favorite for many quilters. Its versatility in prints and colors make it an obvious choice for most projects.

Silk: Luxurious and smooth silk adds an elegant touch. Its reflective quality can introduce a different kind of shine to your quilt.

Linen: Known for its rustic charm, linen can introduce texture and a certain vintage feel.

Batiks: These are cotton fabrics treated with a unique dyeing process that gives them rich, multi-tonal colors and often features unique patterns.

Flannel: Soft and cozy, flannel is perfect for quilts meant for colder seasons.

Deep Dive into Color Theory:

The Color Wheel: Understanding primary, secondary, and tertiary colors can help you identify complementary, analogous, and triadic color schemes.

Warm vs. Cool Colors: Recognizing the emotional impact of colors can guide your choices. Warm colors like red, orange, and yellow evoke feelings of warmth and comfort, while cool colors like blue, green, and purple are calming and serene.

Value and Saturation: Understanding the lightness or darkness (value) and the intensity (saturation) of colors can help in creating depth and contrast in your quilt design.

Choosing Fabrics for Panels:

Scale and Print: While a panel might have a prominent design, the surrounding fabrics should ideally be chosen to complement and not compete with the panel. Consider using smaller prints or solid colors.

Theme Consistency: Ensure the fabric choices resonate with the panel's theme. A woodland-themed panel, for instance, would pair well with fabrics featuring leaves, animals, or forest motifs.

Texture Play: Sometimes, introducing fabrics with varied textures next to the panel can elevate the quilt's tactile appeal.

Complementing Panels with Color Choices:

Highlighting: Use color to draw attention to specific parts of the panel. A patch of blue in a largely warm-colored panel can be emphasized with surrounding blue fabrics.

Mood Setting: Colors set the mood. If a panel features a serene lakeside scene, cool colors like blues and greens can enhance the calm ambiance.

Panel Quilting Mastery

Contrast vs. Harmony: Decide if you want the surrounding fabrics to contrast starkly with the panel or blend harmoniously. Both approaches have their merits and can lead to stunning results.

Expert Tips:

Swatch Test: Before committing to yards of fabric, get swatches. Place them next to your panel and assess how they look in different lighting conditions.

Photograph Your Choices: Sometimes, taking a photograph of your fabric choices laid next to the panel and viewing it from a distance or in grayscale, can give insights into color balance and value.

Trust Your Gut: While theory is invaluable, your personal preference and gut feeling play a significant role. If a fabric or color feels right, even if it doesn't align with conventional wisdom, go for it.

You've dreamed up inspiring quilt layouts showcasing your beautiful panels and prepared your panels for flawless integration. Now, it's time to bring your vision to life by expertly sewing panels along with pieced blocks and setting elements into spectacular quilt tops.

This chapter will cover:

Choosing correct sewing supplies
Preparing panels for sewing
Cutting panels precisely
Marking quilts tops properly
Achieving accurate seam allowances
Keeping panels flat and aligned
Joining panels to blocks
Piecing panels into medallions
Assembling repeating panel quilts
Handling tricky seams and intersections
Finishing flawless quilt tops

Follow these tips to sew stunning quilt tops and incorporate panels with precision and care.

Carolyn Holt

Choosing Sewing Tools

Quality sewing tools prevent frustration when working with panels. Invest in:

Sharp scissors for flawless cutting
A rotary cutter with fresh blades for smooth, slip-free cutting
An acrylic quilter's ruler for transparency while cutting panels
A large cutting mat to fully support large panels
Glass head pins to prevent snagging delicate fabrics
A well-tuned sewing machine capable of fine needle adjustments
Take time to test tools on all fabrics to be quilted and make any adjustments needed to settings or blade sharpness. Dull tools make for jagged cuts and skipped stitches.

Preparing Panels for Sewing

Follow these steps to prep panels for smooth sewing:

Press panels well, including the backs, so fabric lies perfectly flat.
Trim away any selvages or uneven edges to straighten.
Cut panels precisely and according to your planned measurements.
Mark cutting guides on quilt tops only using washable fabric pens or chalk.
Handle panels very gently to prevent any distortion or stretching.

Cutting Panels Precisely

Follow a careful process when using rulers and rotary cutters to slice up pristine panels:

Use an acrylic quilting ruler designed not to slip for best control.
Line up "cut-lines" precisely before cutting to prevent slips.
Hold the ruler firmly in place with even pressure as you cut.
Cut with only a couple of light motions for clean cuts; no sawing.
Change rotary cutter blades frequently for ultra smooth cuts.
Check edges for snags or distortions before removing ruler.
Discard any panels with imperfect cuts rather than risk imperfect piecing.

Panel Quilting Mastery

Take it slowly to perfectly cut panels to your planned dimensions without marring the fabric. Rushing leads to imperfections.

Marking Quilt Tops Properly

Avoid drawing or writing quilting guides or measurements directly on printed panel surfaces. Instead:

Mark quilting guides, like match points, on quilt-top background fabrics.
Use a washable fabric pen or pencil, so marks easily vanish.
Test pens/pencils on panel scraps first, to verify no ink spreads or bleeds.
If needed, use masking or painter's tape as cut guides on panels.
Remove any tape, paper, or markings promptly after cutting/sewing to prevent adhesive residue.
Careful marking prevents marring the surface of your prized panels. Never cut freehand.Precise measurement and cutting guides prevent costly mistakes.

Maintaining Accurate Seam Allowances

With panels, seam allowances become visible, so accuracy matters. Take steps to achieve flawless margins:

Cut panels precisely with 1/4" minimum seam allowance.
Align and cut notches and points, perfectly mirrored, on abutting seams.
Consistently sew, a scant 1/4" from raw edges, for seamless panel joining.
Nest seams and press to one side for flat, inconspicuous transitions.
Press all seam allowances away from panels to avoid shadows through lighter fabrics.
Keep seam allowances consistent and interlocking for professional results when merging panels and blocks.

Keeping Panels Flat and Aligned

Carolyn Holt

Handle panels gently to prevent distortions that will transfer to finished quilts:

Press panels immediately if they become distorted or stretched during handling.
Refold panels, exactly on grain lines, between sewing steps.
Always pin perpendicular to seams within the 1/4" seam allowance only.
Use abundant pins to fully secure panels before sewing.
Never pull panels sideways or skew fabric when joining.
Stop periodically when sewing to re-smooth and re-align panels.
Allow constructed rows to fully rest before joining additional rows.
Take great care when moving panels from your work surface to the sewing machine and back, to avoid tugging or skewing. Panels require gentle, precise handling throughout the construction process for best results.

Piecing Panels into Medallions

Medallion panel quilts allow showcasing a gorgeous central floral, portrait, or scenic print. Surround focal panels with simple pieced borders.

When joining panels point to point with borders, precisely match seam intersections. Mark crucial matched points on the quilt top before sewing. Perfect points and borders frame panels beautifully.

For shaped central panels, like hexagons, carefully join side strips at exact widths to complete the shaped border. Gentle handling prevents distorting bias panel edges.

Piecing Repeat Block Panel Quilts

To join repeating blocks into bold graphic panel quilts, be extremely precise:

Carefully line up printed seams before pinning and sewing.
Measure distances between repeats to maintain proper spacing.
Work to avoid a mismatched measurement between block repeats.
Align edges meticulously during pinning to prevent creeping.

Panel Quilting Mastery

Misalignments become glaringly obvious. Be extremely careful to keep blocks precisely positioned as you sew, pin, and press.

Handling Tricky Panel Seams and Intersections

Take added precautions when sewing:

Adjacent panels - Precisely match abutting motifs and seams.
Panel points - Mark and pin matched seam intersections before sewing.
Panel corners - Sew toward turns slowly, stopping needle down, to pivot sharply.
Bias edges - Prevent stretching by handling gently and pinning abundantly.
Panel intersections - Pin each seam preceding the intersection to avoid movement.
Rush nothing. Inspect from all angles and press frequently when constructing with panels.

Finishing Flawless Quilt Tops

Before declaring your quilt top complete, be sure to:

Remove any marking pens, measurements, tape or paper.
Press entire top using spray starch to set seams.
Steam again from quilt back, to further set stitches.
Inspect closely from all angles in bright light for any flaws or inconsistencies.
Make any needed corrections before quilting errors become permanently sewn into the quilt.
Sign and date completed tops before sandwiching up for quilting.

More Tips for Sewing Flawless Quilts with Panels

Achieving professional results when sewing treasured panels into quilt tops requires extra care and precision. Follow these additional tips:

Choose Smaller Needle Sizes

Carolyn Holt

For detailed panel piecing, opt for finer machine needles size 70 or 80, to stitch perfectly into seam junctures without abrading delicate fabrics. Install a fresh needle before starting any new project.

Stitch with Micro Thread

Reduce thread bulk layers within seams even further by sewing panels together using 100% cotton thread with a weight of 40, rather than the standard 50. Thinner thread tucks seamlessly into seams.

Press Seam Allowances Open

Pressing seams open reduces bulk, which helps perfectly match panel intersections and points. Be diligent, pressing seams flat before opening them to prevent ripples extending into panels.

Approach Intersections with Care

Slow down when approaching seam intersections and points. Pivot with needle down, raise presser foot, and re-pin if needed, to precisely fit elements together before completing seams.

Tweak Tension as Needed

Since panels likely have a different texture and density than partnering fabrics, make tension adjustments as needed, to optimize straight stitching on the finished quilt.

Use a Supreme Slider or Glider

Pucker seams become impossible to correct after sewing. A Teflon slider placed under the fabric layers helps fabrics glide smoothly under the presser foot.

Try a Straight Stitch Throat Plate

Swapping in a special throat plate on your machine with a smaller needle hole prevents fabric from flagging into the hole while perfectly matching points and intersections.

Panel Quilting Mastery

Let Gravity Help

While sewing, allow quilt weight to naturally hang down, keeping the section being sewn flat rather than pulling fabric taut. Gravity helps prevent tunnels and tucks.

Know When to Stop and Fix

If matching key points, panel motifs, or stripe matches proves impossible, it's better to pause, gently remove stitching, and rework areas until every seam lies perfectly flat with all elements aligned.

When using extra diligence while sewing panels, even beginners can achieve breathtaking results. Patience and precision will reward you with heirloom quilts exhibiting flawless workmanship.

Advanced Sewing Techniques for Flawless Panel Integration

Take your panel piecing to the next level with these advanced sewing and pressing techniques:

Grade Seam Allowances

Trim seam allowances gradually narrower as you piece moving away from the focal panel. This reduces bulk concentrically for smoother finishing.

Grade Pressing as Well

On each seam, first press toward the panel foundation, then press allowances open. This helps seams lie perfectly flat while preventing shadows through panels.

Join Borders with Mitered Corners

For sharp contiguous borders around panels, cut adjoining borders with 45 degree miters, and seam corners point to point rather than overlapping perpendicular seams.

Create Invisible Applique

Use organza, iron-on adhesive strips to appliqué panel motif. Be sure to flush edges rather than layering them. Fused edges disappear into the background for a clean dimension.

Apply Edge Starch for Stability

If panels distort along cut edges, lightly mist with starch and press dry on very low heat to set the fibers and prevent stretching when seaming.

Use a Tailor's Ham for Shaping

To set rounded panel edges or seams neatly, press over a tailored ham which mimics body curves rather than a flat surface ironing board.

Try Paper Piece Tricky Seam Allowances

If panel motifs crowd seam allowances, add paper piece foundations to provide sturdy, extended margins for perfect piecing. Tear away after sewing.

Photograph Progress from All Angles

Thoroughly document construction with photos, from all sides during piecing. Photographs help identify any areas that become misaligned or distorted in comparison to previous steps.

With immaculate piecing and pressing, panels integrate seamlessly into quilts. Patience and precision will reward you with timeless heirloom quilts exhibiting breathtaking workmanship.

Chapter 6
Assembling Quilts with Panels

You've sewn up your gorgeous panel quilt top and now it's time to transform it into a finished quilt by assembling the quilted top, batting, and backing into a cohesive whole. Follow these steps to assemble your quilted masterpiece with care:

Prepare Backing Fabric

Prewash backing fabric in warm water using mild detergent and press dry to pre-shrink. Straighten any skewed grain. Plan backing size at least 2" larger than the quilt top on all sides to provide an adequate margin for stretching as you work.

For hand quilting, choose soft firmly woven cottons, like muslin or broadcloth, for easy needle punctures. Machine quilting works best on midweight cotton quilt backings without prominent textures. Poly-cotton blends make budget friendly yet stable backings. Wide backing 108" fabrics simplify assembling large quilts. Avoid low quality, lightweight broadcloths prone to wrinkling. No wrinkles should be evident after pressing.

Join Backing Sections

If your backing fabric isn't wide enough, you'll need to piece sections together to achieve sufficient size. Remove selvages then trim edges square before joining. Cut edges on lengthwise grain for stability.

Panel Quilting Mastery

Overlap and pin wrong sides together offsetting the join from the top's center to prevent weakness where the heaviest quilting will occur. Use long bastion or safety pins, placed perpendicular to edges every 3-4" ensuring edges align snugly from end to end before sewing. Stitch with a 1/2" seam allowance, removing pins just before the presser foot. Press seams open.

Prepare Batting

The choice of batting loft and fiber impacts quilt drape, breathability, and longevity. Cotton and wool are traditional favorites. Blend bats add polyester resilience. Silk, bamboo, and flannel provide ultra softness. Batting also comes in low loft to add with to high loft for plushness. Buy 10% wider batting to prevent stretching as you work. Follow manufacturer's instructions on whether batting may be washed and dried along with finished quilts or requires professional dry cleaning.

Once you've selected batting, press gently all over to straighten any folds or creases. Cut precisely to your finished quilt dimensions.

Layer Quilt Sandwich

With backing and batting prepped, it's time to construct the quilt "sandwich". Work on a smooth, flat surface like a table or mat to prevent distortion. Here's the ideal layering order:

Backing fabric wrong side up
Batting centered on top of backing fabric
Quilt top centered right side up atop batting
Smooth each addition before placing the next layer. Having help makes positioning the layers easier. Ensure all layers lie flat, with edges straight and evenly spaced. Check for wrinkles andr bubbles throughout.

Tip: Place painter's tape X marks at corners through all layers to align as reference points when basting.

Baste Layers Together

Basting temporarily joins the three layers, so you can move the assembled quilt for quilting. Avoid permanent quilting stitches for basting, which may need removing later if you adjust layouts. Try these basting options:

Safety pinning every 3-5" over the surface
Long-running stitches by hand or machine through all layers
Washable glue sprayed onto each layer as it is placed
Paper folded over edges to hold layers or stapled in place
Check areas at seams, edges, and corners for shifting until basting secures all layers together without wrinkles. Add extra basting wherever needed.

Mark Your Quilting Design

With the quilt top now layered and basted, it's time to mark your planned quilting design using washable tools like chalk pencils or erasable pens. You may improvise or follow a marked template for uniform results. Mark in sections as you quilt to prevent smearing complex lines over the surface, e before stitching them.

Here are elements to mark quilting guides for:

Panel outlines to accentuate focal motifs
Registration marks for any border repeats
Background filler patterns in negative spaces
Detailing that enhances and echoes panel designs
Any custom quilting like feathers along borders
Remember to remove all marking lines fully before binding to prevent shadow lines on the quilt face. Avoid using darker permanent markers that may bleed color into fabric when washed. Test markings on all fabrics first.

Prepare Tools for Quilting

Panel Quilting Mastery

Collect any tools you'll need for the quilting process like needles, threads, thimbles, and scissors. Select the best needle for your chosen batting.Avoid large, sharp needles that could tear batting during quilting. Consider 40 or 50 weight micro quilting thread for reduced bulk. Be sure bobbins are filled, needles are fresh, scissors are sharp, and pins/clips plentiful. New gloves help grip slippery silk or metallic threads.

Set Up Your Quilting Frame

Whether using a quilting hoop, frame mounted on a table or full free-standing quilting frame, set up equipment and get comfortable before quilting your layers together. Adjust frame heights and chair position for good posture. Have a pair of scissors near the frame for quick thread snips. Use furniture clamps to stabilize small hoops on tables. For portable lap quilting, be sure legs are fully supported. Do a few warm up quilting lines on a scrap sandwich to make sure everything functions smoothly.

Once your backing, batting, marked, and other required quilt layers are loaded, you're ready to bring them together with your chosen quilting technique. Take your time to create even stitches and uniform quilting lines. Remove any remaining basting once quilting is complete. Finally, trim batting and backing margins even with the quilt top edge, in preparation for neat binding application.

Additional Tips for Flawlessly Assembling Panel Quilts

Achieving perfectly smooth and wrinkle-free quilt assembly takes a few extra steps and care when working through layers. Follow these tips:

Check Batting Shrinkage Rate

Prewash and dry batting samples before use, to determine the amount of shrinkage, so you're sure to purchase adequate yardage for your finished quilt size. Out of all fabrics, cotton shrinks the most, while polyester batting has minimal shrinkage.

Wash Backing Fabrics

Prewash, dry, and press backing fabrics multiple times using your regular detergent and dryer settings until fabric shrinkage stabilizes. This pre-shrinks the quilt before constructing.

Nap Backing Fabrics

Rub the backing fabric pile, in the direction it will hang on the quilt back, so it will lay smoothly. This prevents obvious wash lines on finished quilts due to
 fabric disturbances.
Straighten All Fabric Grains

Before cutting, tug diagonally across the fabric from corner to corner. If it doesn't hang perfectly straight on grain, lightly spray and press again before cutting.

Check Alignment Before Pinning

Lay out all sections from the quilt top before overlapping and pinning to ensure motifs align properly across the quilt top before assembly.

Work from the Center Outward

Smooth layers most carefully from the center outward, so borders don't become stretched or skewed compared to the middle focal panel.

Use Table/Floor Tape

On slick surfaces, secure layers with low tack tape on the underside while positioning. Afterward, pull up tape gently to avoid adhesive residue.

Weight Perimeters

Once centered, place rulers, books, or cans lightly around all the quilt edges before basting to prevent layers creeping, especially along borders.

Don't overstretch layers trying to remove small ripples. Gentle smoothing should relax most wrinkles. Remaining tiny wrinkles will dissipate. t. Relax and enjoy the assembly process!

Panel Quilting Mastery

Flawless Layering and Basting Techniques for Panel Quilts

Proper layering and basting are critical foundations for beautifully quilted panel projects. Follow these steps:

Prepare Assembly Surface

Clear ample surface area to fully lay out all quilt layers together, wrinkle-free. Cover with fresh muslin or batting to prevent snagging. Secure slippery layers with low tack masking tape underside.

Lay Backing Fabric First

Carefully unfold the backing fabric, wrong side up. Smooth from quilt center outward. Check to see if it's squarely positioned. Weight edges so it remains taut and fixed.

Add Batting Second

Unfold batting, starting from the center again. Gently smooth and straighten toward edges, without shifting backing. Avoid overworking batting to prevent bearding.

Top with Quilt Right Sides Up

Unfold completed quilt top, centered precisely over batting, rights side up. Smooth from center outward without skewing previous layers. Edges should align evenly.

Secure Layers Gradually

Working from quilt center out, apply safety pins, glue, or edge weights progressively to affix layers together . Alternate sides, while securing, to distribute tension evenly.

Safety Pin Baste

For traditional safety pin basting, insert pins perpendicularly through all layers every 3-5 inches apart, over the entire surface. Avoid angled pins that stress fabrics.

Glue Baste

For washable glue basting, mist light coats between each layer as you position them. Avoid soaking. Glue bonds layers on contact, but allows repositioning if aligned incorrectly.

Edge Weighting

Place, books, cans, or clamps around quilt perimeters to hold layers flat together once centered and smoothed, without creating piercing holes.

Check Results

Inspect from all angles that layers lie flat together with backing and batting margins extending at least 2 inches past quilt top edges. Make any needed adjustments before final quilting.

Take your time preparing surfaces, aligning, smoothing, and securing layers together properly. Proper basting prevents problem areas.

Chapter 7
Quilting Techniques for Panels

You've selected stunning panels, pieced gorgeous quilt tops, and now it's time to bring everything together with inventive quilting. Decorative quilting enhances panel designs, defines spaces, and unifies the quilt layers into a finished textile. This chapter will guide you through choosing and executing quilting techniques to best showcase your treasured panels.

Topics covered:

Evaluating panel quilting suitability
Selecting hand vs machine quilting
Outlining and echo quilting panel motifs
Background fillers that complement panels
Quilting scale proportionate to panel designs
Highlighting panels with dense quilting
Low contrast threads for spotlighting panels
Free motion quilting with panels
Fussy cut panels and improv quilting
Using panels to guide linear quilting
Twin needle quilting with panels
Advanced panel quilting techniques such as trapunto

Let's explore your many options to make quilting an integral part of the panel design process.

Evaluating Panel Quilting Suitability

Panel Quilting Mastery

Panels aren't uniformly suited to all quilting techniques. Dense, embroidery styleprints become overworked with complex quilting but thrive with simple detailing. Fussy cut motifs pop brightly against low density background fills. Analyze panel style and density to select optimal quilting.

Floral panels allow gently curving, leafy fillers around bouquets.
Striking graphics quilted minimally create bold focus.
Large scale prints suit outlined, gradated fills toward edges.
Blenders integrate smoothly into allover meandering.
Sheers beg for artistic dense quilting to show through.
Whimsy themes inspire playful, illustrative quilting.
Always quilt a couple samples first to verify suitability. Let the panel design guide your quilting choices.

Choosing Hand vs Machine Quilting

Both hand and machine quilting shine with panels but offer distinct advantages:

Hand quilting allows closely for following printed motifs with small, uneven hand stitches which are almost invisible. Intricate fussy cut panels thrive under precise hand quilting. Portability makes hand quilting convenient for large quilts.

Machine quilting excels for dense overall designs, straight lines, and consistency with even stitch length. It quilts faster and is less physically taxing. Home machines suffice for moderate quilting density.

Hybrid approaches combine machine quilting central seams and background fills with hand quilting for detailed panels or borders. Choose the method that best flatters each unique panel project.

Outlining and Echo Quilting Panel Motifs

Selectively tracing and outlining components of the printed panel design with quilting stitches adds deep dimension. Follow these steps:

Mark around key inner motifs with a washable pencil just within the printed edges.

Use a walking foot or contrast thread to sew just inside the marked lines, outlining motifs.

Mark and sew successive lines of echo quilting spaced 1/4" or 1/2" outward to fade the motifs into backgrounds.

Remove all marking lines completely after quilting to prevent shadows.

This technique accentuates focal floral sprays, portrait features, graphic elements, and other panel motifs that catch the eye. It helps key aspects stand out.

Choosing Background Filler Quilting

Background fillers add visual interest and textures around focal printed panels. Select filler quilting motifs that complement panel styles:

Flora/fauna panels inspire curlicues, leaves, feathers, and vines.
Geometrics and modern designs love angular zigzag lines.
Whimsical themes allow playful free motion improv quilting.
Conversational vignettes pair well with meandering trails.
Negative space gets depth from geometric grid lines.
Reproduce panel motifs in fill areas at a different scale.
Let panels guide intuitive filler choices that enhance their beauty.

Quilting at Appropriate Scales

Plan quilting motifs at scales that align aesthetically with the panel print sizes. Tiny stippling looks disjointed against bold oversized florals. Avoid quilting that overwhelms or diminishes the panel impact.

Measure print motif sizes for reference. Giant motifs may cover 24 inches.
Scale filler quilting to about 1/8th of the panel motif size.
Adjust quilting scales gradually from compact positioning near the panel, to larger placement in outer areas.
Maintaining consistent visual weight creates cohesion. Quilting threads should be fine enough for tiny details but sturdy enough for heavy use quilts. Cottons at 40 to 50 weight strike an optimal balance.

Highlighting Panels with Dense Quilting

Panel Quilting Mastery

Frame or accent panel focal points by encircling them with denser quilting than surrounding spaces. This helps panels stand out while allowing filler areas to recede.

Intensely stippled background quilting also boosts the visual impact of focal panels floated within. High density quilting surrounding panels highlights them by contrast.

Low Contrast Thread Colors

Matching top threads closely to panel colors keeps the focus on the printed motifs. Avoid high contrast threads that distract the eye and dominate more nuanced panel hues.

Pick a coordinated monofilament or cotton thread in the same color family as the most prominent panel tones. Low contrast thread color blends away to let the panel shine.

Free Motion Quilting with Panels

Improvisational, free motion quilting based on the panel design itself, helps embed panels into the quilt with artistic originality. Let panels guide the paths of stitched lines.

Replicate shapes and figures in the print with loose free motion echoes. Follow floral stems and leaf veins. Outline key motifs or invent new transitional motifs. Improvise!

Panels inspire artistic quilting tailored to each unique print. Free motion lines flow more organically than geometric templates.
Quilting Fussy Cut Panel Sections

Fussy cut panel motifs surrounded by negative space offer wonderful creative freedom for improvisational quilting. Embellish cut elements using:

Contrasting thread colors for definition
Appropriate motif-inspired outlines
Free motion doodles and scribbles in space
Whimsical or abstract interpretations

Carolyn Holt

Geometric rays radiating from fussy cuts
Each customized panel detail becomes a charming quilt vignette when creatively quilted.

Using Panels to Guide Linear Quilting

Follow straight lines within panel prints to guide linear, machine quilting design paths:

Connect points along floral stems into diagonal grids.
Trace stripes, lattice lines, and web patterns.
Follow piecework patchwork seams.
Outline blocks, stars, or tessellating elements.
Align ruler edges along prints to quilt geometric blocks.
Linear quilting aligned with straight panel motifs adds depth and motion. Play with scale and proximity.

Twin Needle Quilting with Panels

Using a twin needle on your home machine creates two parallel lines of stitching spaced 1/8th to 1/4th inches apart. This offers wonderful options with panels:

Outline panel edges, mimicking binding seam lines.
Shadow print motifs and details just outside their edges.
Insert narrow filler channels between print elements
Add depth when quilting overlapping panel sections.
Define panel vignette sections across quilt tops.
The twin needle allows economical mimicry of time intensive hand work for accenting panels.

Advanced Panel Quilting Techniques

Take your panel quilting to the next level with these striking advanced techniques:

Trapunto - Stuff densely stitched channel quilting around motifs to make them pop in high relief.

Panel Quilting Mastery

Piping - Insert cording into seams around panel contours for extra dimension. Choose cording to match print colors.

Stippling - Handstitched ultra fine popcorn stippling over solid panels provides stunning contrast.

Crosshatching - Meticulously hand stitch or machine crosshatch intricate geometric fills behind bold graphic panels.

Sashiko - Linear, handstitched channels echo panel designs with bold graphic impact.

The perfect panel deserves equally artful quilting. Don't just quilt panels - collaborate with them to create an artistic whole. Match your vision and skills to showcase treasured panels through creative quilting.

More Innovative Quilting Techniques for Enhancing Panels

Take quilting with panels to the next level by exploring more advanced techniques that add striking dimensionality, texture, and visual enhancement:

Dimensional Puffing

Insert polyester or wool batting bits under light topstitching radiating from printed motifs to create subtle dimensional puffing for extra depth. Works well along flower bouquets, organic shapes, and branching details.

Channel Quilting

Dense channel quilting concentrically around key panel focal points and frame them in bold relief. Insert cording before stitching for more definition. Echo channels outward.

Stipple Trapunto

Using fine, curved upholstery needles, sculpt raised shapes by stuffing and shaping batting through the quilt top background around motifs. This will create dramatic, high dimension.

Stitching Shadow Lines

Trace offset echo lines just outside print motifs in slightly darker threads for integrated shadow effects. Add levels of shadow lines for 3D illusion.

Folded Fabric Panel Borders

Insert narrow folded fabric strips or prairie points along straight panel edges to create eyelash fringe effects, floral trims, soft scalloped borders, and more.

Lace Applique Accents

Strategically position wide lace trims, motifs, medallions, or inserts to accentuate floral panels and vignettes using invisible or decorative edge stitching.

Selective Embellishment

Hand stitch eye-catching French knots, seed beads, charms, ribbons, buttons, and bows in concentrated clusters within panel designs or along their seams.

Foiling

Brush fusible foil adhesive over selected motifs, then tint foils for integrated metallic effects. Use heat to adhere foil permanently.

Freezer Paper Stenciling

Cut stencils from freezer paper and position over panels. Stitch through layers to add color or metallic foiling within cut out areas for bold impact.

With so many options, you can quilt panels exactly the way they inspire you. Let your imagination and skills guide creative quilting tailored to match each treasured, printed panel.

Special Considerations for Hand Quilting with Panels

Panel Quilting Mastery

Hand quilting remains a cherished, traditional technique for enhancing detailed printed panels. Follow these tips to maximize success hand quilting panels:

Needles for Hand Quilting Panels

Choose thin, sharp needles between size 10-12 so stitches pierce fabric layers smoothly without tearing fibers or distorting delicate motifs. Avoid large thick needles reserved for heavy seaming.

Hand Quilting Thread Selection

Single ply cotton quilting threads 40 weight or finer, create beautifully tiny hand quilting stitches almost invisibly on panels. Avoid heavy 30 weight threads prone to tangles and knotting. Lightly waxing threads aids smooth stitching.

Marking Hand Quilting Lines

Use only air erasable marking tools like chalk pencils when marking panels. Never risk bleeding ink marks. Test marking tools on all fabrics first. Remove all markings after quilting.

Hand Quilting Stitch Considerations

Aim for tiny straight stitches a consistent 8-10 per inch in size for intricate panel definition. Mark lines at this scale too. Remove knots or tangles promptly to prevent puckering around delicate printed motifs.

Flat Thimbles for Control

Open style leather or plastic thimbles worn on your middle finger improve hand quilting mastery on panels. Unlike closed thimbles, flat thimbles provide excellent fine stitch fingertip dexterity and control.

Hooping Strategies for Hand Quilting

Carolyn Holt

Only hoop portions you are actively quilting to prevent distortion in areas with prolonged hoop pressure. Avoid folding and creasing panel surface fibers by inserting a sheet of tissue paper under the area to be hooped for protection.

Lap Hoops for Large Quilts

Maneuverable lap hoops allow navigating large quilts to stitch detailed regions comfortably without basting entire tops. Position hoops precisely before stitching panel segments.

Needle Positioning Over Panels

Insert needles immediately adjacent to marked lines without ever piercing printed motifs to avoid damaging panel surfaces. This takes extreme care and practice.

Perfecting Your Stitch

Practice consistently sized straight stitches endlessly, on fabric scraps until motion becomes natural before stitching panels. Knotless starting, smooth rocking motion, and even tiny stitches prevent marring panels.

Pressing During Hand Quilting

Avoid pressing quilted sections until stitching is complete to prevent disturbing delicate applied stitches. Press finished motifs individually on the quilt back using a padded surface like a Turkish towel.

With close attention to tools and technique, hand quilting elevates panels to extraordinary works of textile art stitch by stitch. Pursue perfection - the results merit time invested!

Mixed Media Quilting with Panels Photo Gallery

Panel Quilting Mastery

Quilt artists are increasingly exploring mixed media techniques to integrate non-textile elements with traditional quilting for more organic, dimensional fiber art. Combining painting, printing, surface design, photography, and found materials with panels, opens new frontiers of creative possibilities.

This photo gallery features examples of captivating mixed media panel quilts along with insights on processes and materials behind the artistry. Prepare to be inspired!

Ocean Waves Mixed Media Quilt by Aliza Keller

This atmospheric quilt mimics the mesmerizing movement of ocean waves. The quilter digitally printed custom coordinated fabric panels with gradations of blue. Free motion machine embroidery and bobbin work form abstract waves, layered with sheer organza overlays. Dimensional sheer fabric folded shapes create foamy wave crests. Hand stitching attaches ribbon "seaweed" embroidered with beads. Heavy free motion quilting enhances texture. Unconventional materials capture the spirit of water.

Desert Heat Mixed Media Art Quilt by Mel Beach

The artist hand dyed gradient sunset panels to invoke desert skies, then overlaid a digitally printed silhouette panel of saguaro cacti. Orange mesh and cheesecloth form undulating sand dunes. Intricate machine appliqué cacti and embroidered flowers pop brightly against the subdued backdrop. Metallic overlays add shimmer, while dense free motion quilting heightens dimension. Unexpected materials form a bold dry landscape.

Steampunk Mechanical Panel Quilt by Aliza Keller

This quilt combines digitally printed panels of metallic gears, watch parts, and diagrams with matte solid black fabric. Freezer paper stencils allowed printing metallic foils selectively onto the black background in detailed geometric designs. The quilter used dense stitch-in-the-ditch outlining and heavy background textures to heighten machine-like precision. Watch parts are sewn on with exposed puffy trapunto. The unconventional combination captures mechanical vibrancy.

Carolyn Holt

Night Sky Aurora Borealis Quilt by Lisa Walton

Deep space photography panels are overlaid with glitter organza and metallic foils radiating light like the aurora borealis. Bobbin work swirls galactic clouds of ribbon and threads. Shredded black sari silk creates dimensional darkness. Dense quilting stabilizes while adding nebula-like texture. Free motion quilting spirals outward in cosmic waves. Grounding solids frame the celestial explosion. Unexpected materials form cosmic beauty.

Under the Sea Mixed Media Panel Quilt by Soma Roy

The quilter digitally printed coral reef panel designs onto quilting cotton, then gave dimensional life by thread sketching aquatic plants in bobbin work. She embroidered whimsical details like fish, seashells, and bubbles with metallic threads. Layers of sheer tulle and chiffon form gentle waves and sea foam textures. Trapunto corals pop in relief. Silky soft blues capture the mystery of the deep.

Sunset Mesa Art Quilt by Carol E. Anderson

This lovely quilt overlays solid color panels with vigorous hand dyed brushwork, forming brilliant sunset skies over a mesa. Scraps of natural silk are twisted and fused into tumbleweed shapes. Dense stitching heightens texture in the mesa. Improvised prairie points become dotted wildflowers. Free motion quilting echoes the brush strokes, and unrestrained mixed media form dramatic vistas.

Digital Forest Panel Quilt by Aliza Keller

The quilter digitally printed panels with photographs of a mystical forest, then quilted organic textures like leaves, vines, and bark with heavy thread painting and bobbin work. Green and brown sheer overlays heighten dimension. Embroidery and metallic foil accents add magical glow effects. Dimensional prairie points become fluttering moths, and dense free motion quilting heightens shadows and shapes. These simple materials create enchanted, wooded intrigue.

Ocean Waves Mixed Media Quilt by Carol E. Anderson

Panel Quilting Mastery

Abstract waves tumble across this quilt in thickly stitched wavy bands of gradient blue hues on panels. Bobbin work, swirls supply texture like sea foam. Silky organza and chiffon, form the waterfall wave edges cascading downward. Densely quilted rays emanate outward mimicking ocean spray. Ribbons stitched in rivulets add frothy movement, and heavy machine quilting creates liquidity. Free flowing materials help to invent waves in the fiber.

Metropolis Pixel Panel Quilt by Violet Craft

This modern urban quilt fuses solid high contrast panels with large-scale pixelated, cityscape imagery printed on cotton panels. Geometric high-rise shapes are outlined with stiff interfacing then zigzag stitched for pop. Tiny machine embroidered windows add city lights. Improvised folded fabric strips join building tops. Dense meandering fills the background space. An unexpected whimsical touch softens urban, melded media.

Desert Landscape Mixed Media Quilt by Lisa Walton

Photographic panels capture desert vistas in rich sepia tone,s then get overlaid loosely with torn silk chiffon rags, stitched in circular wind patterns. Twisting fibers, secured with dense quilting, form rugged arroyos. Fragments of hand dyed cheesecloth blend into sun baked mesas. Metallic accents glint light off rippled sands, whileatural textures symbolize the raw beauty of deserts.

These astonishing mixed media quilts demonstrate the creative frontiers that open when panels interplay with painting, printing, photography, embellishment, and imaginative materials. Artistic spirit transcends fabric and threads. We hope these visionary examples inspire your own panel possibilities!

Carolyn Holt

Chapter 8

Borders, Sashing, and Settings for Panel Quilts

Creative borders, sashing, cornerstones, and setting blocks are wonderful co-stars supporting focal quilt panels. This chapter will guide you in selecting colors, dimensions, and piecing methods to make settings that enhance your stellar panels.

Topics covered:

Evaluating border roles like framing, expanding, complementing
Selecting straight grain borders for stability
Sizing borders appropriately to panel scales
Cutting precise border strips accurately
Joining borders with color coordinated corners
Adding straight sashing between blocks
Figuring precise sashing dimensions
Incorporating colorful cornerstones
Piecing creative scalloped and curved borders
Using piano key, stub, and sawtooth sashing
Cutting and joining mosaic frame settings
Mixing patchwork frames with panels
Printing custom, coordinated border fabric
Incorporating panels into borders
Creating continuity with border motifs
Follow along to demystify calculating and constructing the perfectly coordinated borders and settings to spotlight your sensational panels!

Evaluating Border Roles

Before selecting border prints, assess what roles you want them to play relation to the featured panel:

Framing – Neutral, receding borders frame and draw attention inward to panels as focal points.

Expanding – Borders widen the quilt canvas to house central panels with breathing room.

Complementing –Tonally harmonious border prints reinforce panel colors.

Augmenting - Contrasting border hues and prints energetically interact with panel motifs.

Transitioning - Graduated borders create visual bridges between panels and outer settings.

Knowing border purposes guides print, scale, and color choices.

Selecting Straight Grain Borders

Piecing borders on the crosswise straight grain of the fabric keeps them flat, straight and square as their lengthwise edges are vulnerable to stretching. Straight borders properly frame squared panel edges.

Cut border strips the exact measurement required plus 1/4" seam allowance. Don't trim strips post sewing or re-cut inaccurate segments to match others. Measure meticulously, cut accurately, and gently handle strips for flawless flat borders.

Sizing Border Widths Thoughtfully

Plan border widths suited to panel sizes and the quilt's overall dimensions. Excessively narrow borders shrink the visual focus of anchor panels. Overly wide ones overwhelm and diminish them. Consider:

Small scale or repeat panels warrant narrow borders from 2"-4" so details aren't lost.
Large central focal panels may suit 6-10" borders to provide breathing room.
Multiply panel size by .10 - .25 to calculate ideal border widths.

Panel Quilting Mastery

Gradually decrease border widths further from the focal panel toward outer edges.

Repeat border strips will multiply the chosen width to desired outer size.

Take measurements from finished quilt tops, not estimated final sizes, which may shift. Craft proportional balance between panels and borders.

Cutting Precise Borders

Cut every border strip individually to exactly measured dimensions against quilt tops-never assume pre-cuts are perfectly accurate. Here's an accurate cutting method:

Measure quilt top width from edge to edge across the middle. Cut side borders to this length.

Measure the quilt top from top to bottom across the middle. Cut top/bottom borders to this length.

Align border strips precisely perpendicular to the fabric grain and straight of grain ruler markings.

Use a rotary cutter and straight edge ruler to cut precisely.

Repeat for each border strip needed.

Handle strips very gently to prevent stretching before sewing.

Meticulous measuring and cutting prevents inaccuracies rippling through border alignment.

Joining Borders with Color Coordinated Corners

For perfectly mitered borders with continuous color flow at corners, cut and sew individual cornerstone squares between borders.

Cut 4 same-size squares, matching border print.

Sew side borders between cornerstones, then to top and bottom borders.

Nest seams and press borders outward.

Flawlessly matched, mitered corners lend to a panel's polished, professional framing. Continuous color minimizes attention drawn to corners.

Adding Straight Borders

For straight-set borders with 90-degree corners, simply sew borders perpendicular to quilt tops and between contrasting borders. But first...

Measure full widths and lengths of quilt tops very precisely.
Carefully cut straight grain border segments to exact measurements.
Pin borders to quilt tops, matching midpoints and ends accurately.
Sew one side first, then the opposite. Next, sew remaining sides neatly, abutting corners.
Press borders outward.
Measuring twice and gentle handling prevents distortion. Check right angles at corners.

Figuring Sashing Dimensions

How to calculate straight sashing strips running between blocks and borders:

Measure block width/length from raw edge to raw edge across middle.
Add 1/4" for each seam allowance.
Divide desired finished sashing width by this number to determine how many sashing strips needed.
Multiply sashing strip number by unfinished width + allowances for cut size.
Repeat to calculate horizontal and vertical sashing sizes separately.
Precisely cut, equal width sashing, keeps panel layouts square.

Adding Colorful Cornerstones

For sashing with pops of color, cut small squares to match or contrast sashing strips, and sew between intersection blocks.

Cut squares equal in finished width to sashing strips.
Sew strips and squares together into rows first.
Sew sashing rows between quilt blocks/panels.
Adorning sashing with cornerstones, dresses up panel layouts.

Piecing Specialty Border Shapes

Panel Quilting Mastery

For added flair, piece borders in rounded, scalloped, or jagged zigzag edge shapes.

Scalloped borders – Mark and cut waves using templates. Join rows point to point, and add straight sashing.

Zigzag borders – Mark peaked points on border strips and angle cut. Position peaks opposite valleys and sew angled seams.

Novelty shapes make plain straight borders and sashing feel fresh again.

Printing Custom Borders

Many online services will custom print photo uploaded seamless border repeats. Consider custom printing yardage replicating the exact panel print design or motifs to integrate panels visually into borders.

Coordinate these custom border fabrics with panels for perfectly harmonious continuity showcasing the printed motifs.

Incorporating Panels into Borders

Why relegate panels only to quilt centers? Integrate cut panel sections into pieced borders too.

Slice large scale panels into border block inserts between sashing. Utilize repetitive all over panels as a straight border. Fussy cu,t then mix and match panel sections into patchwork border rows.

Expand thinking beyond conventional uses of panels in traditional border roles.

Creating Continuity with Border Motifs

Bring cohesion to panel quilts with sashing and decorated cornerstones using similar motifs as the central panel prints.

Embellish plain setting strips with:

Printed appliques in matching motifs
Stenciled or stamped shapes
Attached fabric picotage, rickrack, or lace
Dyed or overprinted patterns

Echoing themes in subtle ways throughout provides satisfying continuity.

With limitless options for enhancing panels through coordinated borders, sashing, and cornerstones, you can frame treasured panels to perfection. Next, let's explore show stopping quilting designs to make them shine.

More Tips for Creative Borders and Settings with Panels

Take borders, sashing, and settings to the next level with these advanced tips for showcasing quilt panels:

Curved Pieced Borders

For fluid curved borders, draw gentle wavy lines on paper templates. Add seam allowances. Cut and pin curved strips concave or convex. Perfect curves frame panels dynamically.

Mosaic Borders

Make mosaic style borders by tessellating small fussy cut panel motifs set together like tiles within structured straight or zigzag sashing.

Framed Panel Borders

Cut and frame same-size panel sections in colored sashing. Sew together into a column to make a repeating panel border. Showcase the print.

Alternating Sashing

Panel Quilting Mastery

Make plain sashing exciting by periodically alternating sections of contrasting colors, varied widths, or different directional orientations for modern energy.

Sashing with Crossovers

Narrow sashing strips that intersect each other at various angles create bold graphic framing for central focal panels. High contrast pops.

Improvisational Pieced Borders

Let go of structure and improvise free form patchwork border rows featuring fragmented fussy cut panel motifs in asymmetrical off-kilter arrangements.

Multi-Panel Borders

Align a series of different complementary panel prints edge-to-edge to make kaleidoscopic borders. Combine botanicals, geometrics, florals, stripes, and more.

Shaped and Mitered Sashing

Angle cut patchwork sashing strips to create precise angled miters at intersections for show stopping geometric definition along with color flow.

Sashing and Border Motifs

Make all setting pieces graphically bold by decorating them with linear quilting, ribbon appliquéing, bead work, embroidery, or charms echoing panel motifs.

Woven Borders

Mimic woven tapestries by interlacing contrast color sashing over and under through border posts for intricate textural effects.

With thoughtful color, print, and construction selection, borders and sashing become so much more than just structural afterthoughts. They elevate panels to masterpiece status.

Advanced Techniques for Elevating and Integrating Borders

Moving beyond basic strips and squares, explore advanced techniques for borders and sashings that seamlessly integrate with focal quilt panels:

Printed Panel Extensions

Commission wider custom yardage printed with extended motifs to perfectly match and continue panel designs outward into continuous borders.

Invisible Fussy Cut Borders

Hide fussy cut seams for smooth transitions between panels and borders by matching motifs precisely, then sewing with tiny hidden stitch width on rear.

Cross Hatching Borders

Add the illusion of depth and dimension by cross-hatching linear machine quilting along border segments in gradually widening gaps moving outward from panels.

Shadowed Borders

Mimic layered dimension by threading twin needles on your home machine to sew shadow lines just outside border seams, which echo their shapes.

Mitered Grid Borders

Instead of strips, piece borders from segments with angled column ends, creating color shifted stepped edges surrounding panels.

Panel Quilting Mastery

Tassel Border Trims

Frame panels with a softly tufted touch by sewing on purchased or handmade fabric tassel garlands along inner and outer border edges.

Crystal Pleated Borders

For sparkling borders, sandwich crystal pleating between sheer panels and backing, before quilting layers together along border sections.

Folded Fabric Borders

Attach folded fabric border strips overlapping inner and outer edges for tailored self-binding effects in coordinated or contrasting prints.

Printed Binding Fabric

Print custom fabric yardage scaled exactly to your quilt binding width and decorate it with panel design elements for flawless continuity.

With creatively integrated borders and sashing, your prized panels transform from fabric to captivating focal points. Elevate their beauty by every thoughtful design decision.

Innovative Embellished Borders and Settings

Completely customize the style of your panel quilt by embellishing borders, sashing, and cornerstones with unique artistic touches:

Dimensional Hand Appliquéing

Appliqué personalized motifs, flowers, vines, or shapes using dimensional techniques like ruching, prairie points, ribbon work
  and more.

Metal Embossed Borders

Use metal embossing techniques over custom printed sashing strips decorated with large scale floral motifs from the quilt panel for integrated glitz.

Beaded Borders

Frame panels beautifully with beaded trims or hand stitch glowing beads in scalloped waves, dangling fringe or floral sprays along straight or shaped borders.

Fabric Manipulated Borders

Ruffle, pleat, slash, gather, or otherwise manipulate solid border strips or printed panel sections for artistic textural borders with lots of movement.

Painted and Dyed Borders

Over-dye, hand paint, airbrush, marble, ombre, or otherwise artistically alter sashing and border strips to harmonize with colorful panels through similar pigment.

Sculptural Borders

Mix media by sculpting dimensional clay, paper, polymer clay, wood, metal, or glass border embellishments to frame panel focal points distinctively.

Embroidered Motifs and Monograms

Add personalization by adorning borders with custom embroidered motifs, letters, dates and decorative accents using high sheen specialty threads.

Fabric or Lace Appliqued Overlays

Frame central panels by overlaying shaped fabric scallops, medallions, or custom motifs using appliqué or lace overlay techniques for delicate contrast.

Panel Quilting Mastery

Crystal or Sequin Accents

Make straight sashing and cornerstone settings sparkle by embellishing them with selective handstitched, clear, colored, and opalescent crystals or sequins.

Even simple settings become remarkable when thoughtfully adorned. Elevate your treasured quilt panel masterpiece with loving personalization through embellished accents!

Chapter 9
Embellishing and Customizing Panels

Your beautiful printed quilt panels provide the launching point to let creativity soar through artistic embellishment. This chapter explores endless options for enhancing panels with dimensional details, surface design, mixed media arts, fabric manipulation and other innovative customizing techniques.

Topics covered:

Evaluating panel suitability for embellishment
Choosing compatible fabric manipulation techniques
Dimensional embellishments like buttons, beads, ribbons
Attaching decorative trims and fabric features
Cutting intricate motifs with overlay applique
Quilting embellished panels densely to show off details
Options for coloring and dying base panels
Collaging papers, photos, or fabric onto panel surfaces
Incorporating creative embroidery and thread painting
Applying foil and crystalline accents over panel motifs
Using inked printing for stamped patterns and lettering
Painting and fabric marking to alter panel surfaces
Partial coloring with ice, snow, or wax resist methods
Adhering found object and photo transfers onto panels
Free motion machine couching with heavy threads and yarns
Sculpting panels over dimensional forms for shaping
Distressing panels through fraying, tearing, iron texturing
Protecting embroidered panels with wash away stabilizers

Let's explore all you can do to make each panel uniquely yours through creative embellishment!

Carolyn Holt

Evaluating Panels for Embellishment

Heavily inked or dense printed panels compete visually with surface embellishment. Choose panels wisely:

Batiks take dye and paint well without bleeding colors.
Sheer and lightly printed panels best show off dense quilting.
Sparse conversational panels pop with collage and mixed media.
Blank linen panels offer the ultimate embellishment canvas.
Test pens, paints, and glues first, on scraps across the panel design, to ensure they interact as desired.

Choosing Fabric Manipulation Techniques

Panels dimensionalized through fabric manipulation gain texture and capture shadows for added depth. Consider:

Ruching, pleating, gathering, crinkling, fringe making
Trapunto stuffed channels surrounding printed elements
Slashing and rejoining panel motifs irregularly
Overlapping spiraled whirls flowing outward from motifs
Pressing raised textures like rings, dots, and lines around designs
Manipulate fabrics to complement panel personality, from subtle to dramatic.

Applying Dimensional Embellishments

Dimensional designs handstitched or glued onto panel surfaces infuse artistic spirit:

Buttons, beads, sequins, baubles, and jewels
Ribbons, lace, rickrack, piping, and trims
Fabric leaves, flowers, circles, and vines
Ornaments, charms, found objects, and keepsakes
Metal, wood, clay, or glass handmade elements
Clustering intricate details around prints and in negative space adds depth.

Panel Quilting Mastery

Dense Quilting to Showcase Dimensionality

Heavily quilt up to and around appliques, charms, buttons, and raised panel areas. Dense matrices make embellishments pop while securing them in place long-term.

Use monofilament or invisible thread with extra top tension to sink embellishment threads and avoid snagging during the quilting process. Check tops frequently for any dragging before completing intricate quilting.

Dyeing Panels

Dye panels before or after construction for integrated hues or ombre gradients. Try these methods:

Ice dyeing around tied off motif centers
Airbrush spraying gradients across panels
Dye pots with dipping forms like leaves or lace
Ink jet printer feed, dye sublimation all over or in strips
Solar silk painting for atmospheric gradients
Custom yardage screen printing repeats matching panels
Partial dyeing leaves blank areas for quilting brilliance. Set saturated dyes by heat steaming or rinsing.

Printing Panels

Use printmaking techniques to apply patterns and imagery directly onto blank or softly printed panels:

Stamp pads, handmade stamps, erasers, or linocut blocks
Stencils with sponged pigments, resist pastes or inks
Rubber cement or gelatin plate transfers of photos or ephemera
Thermofax or block printing with textile inks
Linoleum carved erasers for small repeating motifs all over
Adhere sheer overlays like tulle before printing for hazy effects. Heat set pigments between layered tea towels.

Carolyn Holt

Collaging Panels

Build up eclectic textures by adhering layers of fabrics, papers, photos, and found scraps to panels:

Sheer fabric layers give gauzy dimension.
Snippets of old letters or ledger papers add history.
Photocopy transfers of vintage imagery using gel medium.
Scraps of maps, music sheets, doilies, or lace add stories.
Attach photos, buttons, pins, stickers or charms.
Free motion quilting ties down collage layers while adding more interest.

Thread Painting and Embroidery

Bring exceptional dimension by stitching, couching and needle painting with threads directly on panels:

Draw and fill shapes with embroidery stitches by hand or machine.
Sketch paisleys, vines, and scrolls swirling from motifs.
Use bobbin stitching and thread painting for shaded effects.
Couch yarns, ribbon, cords, and textures in wavy lines.
Use Trapunto embroider to channel, then stuff to puff around appliques.
Color blended threads enhance dimension. Avoid overly dense embroidered areas where quilting becomes problematic.

Metallic Foiling

Attaching metallic leafing, foils, or luster inks adds light catching shimmer to select panel motifs:

Brush fusible metallic foils over stenciled areas, then heat set with an iron.
Use adhesive transfer sheets to apply gold leaf details.
Paint motifs with interference or holograph colors.
Sponge pearlized pigments, like mica powder, mixed with gel medium.
Foiling draws light to highlighted aspects of panels for drama. Enhance with machine quilting embellished sections.

Panel Quilting Mastery

Free Motion Machine Couching

You can machine couch decorative threads and yarns through the panel surface for bold texture:

Adjust tension, so the needle jumps over embellishing threads.
Attach threads and yarns to machine with low tack masking tape.
Gently guide threads to form designs withmachine stitches.
Try zigzags, flames, and swirls, following printed motifs,
Free motion couching allows drawing with threads. Secure well with closely quilted echoing.

Sculpting Panels

For organic art, sculpt panels by:

Draping over curved solid forms like balls or bowls
Inserting batting between top and back to create raised relief
Compressing certain sections under heavyweight books or pressing
Ruching, pleating, and ruffling fabric around printed motifs
Sculptural shaping casts realistic shadows and contours. Embrace puckers and wrinkles, adding dimensionality. Drape freely without over-manipulating.

Partial Coloring Techniques

Dye or mark panels selectively using painterly resist techniques:

Rubber cement or wax outlines safeguard blank motifs.
Plastic stencils or tape, shields defined spaces.
Wrapped elastics, threads, or clamps compress protection
Ice and saline dyeing reserves un-dyed sections
Preserve charming blank spots amidst saturated colors. Set dyes then rinse away barriers.

Distressing Panels

Add vintage allure by artificially aging and distressing pristine panels before or after constructing quilts:

Tea stain for antique sepia tones.
Spritz water and crinkle for wrinkle effects.
Gently fray raw edges with seam rippers.
Use fine sandpaper or emery boards to thin distressed spots.
Hammer metal stamps or inked lace for imprinted patterns.
Distressing provides depth and visual complexity. Go slowly and carefully monitor effects. Avoid over-softening structured patterns.

Panels present prime canvases for every embellishment technique. Take inspiration directly from the printed motifs. Turn basic panels into spectacular fiber art!

More Innovative Panel Embellishing Ideas

Take surface embellishment to the next level by exploring these additional unique techniques for customizing and enhancing quilt panels:

Liquid Resist Marking

Make batik-style designs by painting liquid latex resist along desired motif edges. Dye panel and dry fully. Then, wash away the resist to reveal reserved blank shapes.

Inked Edge Highlighting

Trace and define select printed elements by backfilling their edges with sponged India ink. Use stiffened stencils to prevent seepage.

Rubbed Pigment Antiquing

Dab oil pastels, chalk, or dry brush inks heavily over raised surface textures. Gently wipe away to leave color concentrated primarily in indentations and seam lines.

Adhering Found Objects

Affix meaningful trinkets like watch parts, dominoes
, game pieces, or carved, wooden pieces using strong glue or fabric welding to make symbolic statements.

Panel Quilting Mastery

Partial Overdyeing

Mask off matrix printed areas with tape, then dye surrounding backgrounds in contrasting hues. Remove tape to reveal kaleidoscopic color blocking.

Discharge Printing

Use bleach discharge pastes, applied through stencils or stamps, to selectively remove patches of color and expose underlayers.

Integrated Surface Piecing

Overlap scraps of coordinating prints strategically, as collage inserts, within areas of the panel design for extra tailoring.

Windowpane Overlays

Softly overlay panels with sections of sheer organza or panels featuring squared cutouts to create a hazy framed dimension around motifs.

Pressed Texture Embossing

Enhance solid panels by heat embossing repetitive geometric textures through custom-carved embossing plates.

Advanced Techniques for Panel Embellishment

For expert panel enhancement, explore these sophisticated techniques requiring specialized supplies and studio space:

Screen Printing

Professionally screen print additional colors, patterns, and overlays matched specifically to the panel design either directly onto panels or onto separate fabrics to be appliquéd.

Encaustic Painting

Carolyn Holt

Brushstroke encaustic, beeswax enriched paints, melted and blended directly onto the surface to offer depth, transparency, layering, and intriguing crackled texture.

Metal Leaf Application

Adhere lustrous gold, silver, and copper leafing permanently, using specialized size adhesives and tools. Antique patinas further enhance metallics. Protect your creation with varnish.

TGV Colour Vapor Application

Using specialized Thermochromic Gas-Vapor pigments, airbrush temperature reactive colors onto panels that shift and evolve, according to ambient heat and cold.

Digital Textile Printing

Work with fine art textile printing services to digitally print photos, artworks, or overlays scaled to the exact panel dimensions with vivid photorealism using large format textile printers.

Archival Transfer Printing

Adhere imagery, like vintage photographs, with no background using your home inkjet printer and specialty transfer mediums that block backgrounds from bonding to fabric.

Acid Etching

Use etching creams safe for fabric to "burn" away layers of color on dense panel surfaces revealing underlayers in decorative aged distress.

Fine Silverwork Embroidery

Panel Quilting Mastery

Importantly highlight key details and motifs by expertly hand embroidering them using smooth pure silver wire and tiny cast silver beads withspecialized needles.

With the right tools and techniques, embellishing panels opens whole new realms of creative possibilities. The printed fabric becomes just the starting canvas for singular works displaying your vision.

Special Considerations for Embellished Panel Quilting

When quilting elaborate embellished panels, take steps to protect fine details from stitching disturbances:

Stabilize Fabric Around Embellishments

Stitch closely around attached buttons, charms, appliqués, and raised areas using short stitches and a lightweight stabilizer underneath, to set embellishments in place before general quilting.

Invisible and Monofilament Thread

Coordinating clear or transparent nylon thread becomes nearly invisible against panels, so stitches avoid distracting from or catching on delicate surface embellishments.

Quilt More Densely Near Embellishments

Increase quilting line density around and alongside dimensional elements to secure them firmly within quilting valleys, without having to stitch directly over the top of them.

Cover Shank Buttons

Carolyn Holt

Protect delicate glass, ceramic, and plastic buttons from cracking or scuffing under the applied pressure of quilting, by covering shanks with small fabric caps secured with flexible, washable glue before attaching buttons.

Avoid Dragging the Feed Dogs

If adjustable, raise feed dogs incrementally to lightly skim over but not catch on embellishment edges. Too low risk thread snarls. Check tension.

Use Supreme Sliders

Supreme sliders, placed between the machine throat plate and fabric surface, allow dimensional embellishments to slide smoothly under foot pressure without catching or distorting.

Check Needle Clearance

Ensure the needle has adequate clearance on all sides when centered precisely over thick spots like buttons and charms, using the handwheel to avoid collisions or breakage.

Hand Guide Around Intricacies

For extra insurance, hand guide, steer, and turn the quilt sandwich while holding embellishments safely out of the path just ahead of the machine foot.

With care, your treasured embellished panels become quilted keepsakes rather than casualties. Prior, proper, planning prevents puckers, breakage, and tears!

Chapter 10

Panel Quilting for Modern and Trendy Projects

In addition to traditional bed quilts, creative quilters are showcasing panels in home décor items, accessories, wearable art, and more. This chapter explores fresh ideas for transforming panels into unique quilted projects with contemporary flair.

Topics covered:

Modern panel wall hangings and minimalist quilts
Quilted pillows and cushions highlighting graphic panels
Tote bags and zippered pouches featuring fabric panel designs
Turning clothing and accessories into personalized statement pieces with panels
Using panels to create artsy abstract quilted sculptures
Panel pet beds and pet accessories for furry friends
Incorporating panels into quilted storage baskets and boxes
Making baby quilts with whimsical and educational panels
Holiday panels for festive quilted decorations and stockings
Idea journals with interchangeable quilted panel covers
Creating memory and photo quilts with personalized panels
Upcycling panel remnants into jewelry, coasters, and small quilts

Follow along for techniques, inspirations and patterns to discover exciting new possibilities showcasing your fabulous panels!

Modern and Minimalist Panel Quilts

Sleek, minimalist panel quilts using bold graphics or solid color fabrics, exude chic modern style. Follow these tips:

Choose graphic or abstract prints with simple color stories.

Panel Quilting Mastery

Frame panels in very narrow solid or black sashing.
Quilt linear paths, echoing the straight lines in print designs.
Use black binding for crisp edges and contemporary finish.
Hang small panel quilts on the wall without visible rods or trimming.
Scale up supersized pattern details into stunning quilts.
Add selective pops of neon or metallics for unexpected zing.
Simple, refined elements keep the full focus on the gorgeous panel designs.

Quilted Pillows with Panels

Fun, quirky, or meaningful printed panels make excellent focal points for accent pillows. For tailored pillows:

Cut 18-24" panels to desired shape.
Back with black or bold color, coordinated solid
Bind edges neatly using 1/4" batting strip inserts
For a more dimensional free-form look:

Fussy cut elements to appliqué on pillow bases.
Print titles or quotes directly onto pillow fronts.
Oversize and overlap fan favorite panels for playful combinations.
Create out-of-the-box panels with unexpected, unconventional shapes.
Panels pump up plain pillows into personalized art objects.

Tote Bags and Pouches Showcasing Panels

Totes and zip bags designed around printed panels provide portable ways to keep favorite fabric art motifs close at hand.

For sturdy quilted tote bags:

Piece together bold, complementary panel sections for bags.
Use black webbing, leather, or corded handles for a modern edge.
Bind top edges, andinsert boxed bottoms for structure.

For softer collapsible pouches:

Back full panels with batting only.
Bind outer edges with rounded corners.

Add wrist straps, drawstrings, or tab closures.

Quilting protects and reinforces delicate panel bags for lasting enjoyment.

Wearable Panel Quilting

Why reserve panels only for beds and walls? Cut, embellish, and quilt them into stunning wearable art too!

Place graphic panels center stage on vest fronts or jacket backs.

Fashion artsy, heirloom memory quilts into capes.

Appliqué meaningful motifs onto pockets or collar tips.

Create couture by framing panels in strips of coordinating prints.

Bind and quilt panels into lightweight infinity scarves.

Decorate jean jackets and denim with iron-on appliquéd panel motifs.

Design strappy sundresses or tiered skirts featuring symmetrical prints.

Artsy Abstract Panel Quilting

Think beyond traditional rectangles. Get creative splicing and rearranging panels into abstract, sculptural fiber art.

Slice narrow bias panel strips to weave into wavy, organic, free form shapes.

Overlap skewed asymmetric fragments in dense collaged textures.

Merge sliced printed strips into new, non-objective compositions.

Attach irregular folded and twisted fabric bits onto abstract wall art.

Wrap quilted panel pieces over rustic wooden hoops and hangers.

Layer translucent panels and shreds for multidimensional arrangements.

Cutting up panels breaks all the rules,and wonderful original art emerges!

Themed Pet Beds and Accessories

Surprise your furry friends with plush quilted beds and toys sporting playful or stylish panels designed just for them.

Panel Quilting Mastery

For pet beds:

Back panels featuring pets, bones, polka dots, or posies with flannel.
Quilt lightly and bind edges using child safe binding techniques.
Add ties or straps to secure slipcover beds to crates neatly.

For pet bandanas, toys, and treats:

Use animal print, comic, or food theme panels.
Bind around edges. Trim and notch for ties.
Stuff small panel pieces with catnip or treats, and bind edges.

Pets love their custom quilted accessories as much as you do!

Quilted Storage Baskets and Boxes

Sturdy storage solutions look extra special when quilted from panels on the exterior.

For large laundry baskets:

Panel sides with sturdy decoded fabric box bottoms.
Bind top edges, and add leather handles for easy toting.

For covered tissue boxes:

Wrap top and four sides in coordinating panels.
Quilt the exterior lightly, andbind edges neatly.

For fabric cubbies, pouches, and boxes:

Use panels on the exterior, and line interiors with cotton prints.
Box stitch the corners, and bind box edges.

Baby Quilts with Cute and Educational Panels

Carolyn Holt

Sweet panels featuring animals, storybook characters, and shapes entertain and educate little ones while accenting their room.

For playful baby quilts:

Back whimsical panels with cotton or flannel for coziness.
Frame panels simply to maintain focus on central designs.
Add touches like appliquéd initials or names for personalization.

For sensory stimulating taggies:

Adorn infant taggy quilts with peekaboo flaps, crinkly fabrics, bells, and varied textures surrounding baby friendly panels.

For activity quilts:

Appliqué tactile bits like zippers, buttons, pockets, peekabos, and ephemera to alphabet, number, or color panels

Babies love cooing over cheerful fabric panel imagery while learning!

Festive Holiday Panels

Celebrate every season by transforming festive holiday panels into home decor and handmade gifts.

For seasonal throws:

Back red and green Christmas panels, andbind the edges.
Add motifs like holly and berries using embroidery or fusible appliquéing.

For stockings:

Cut and sew main stocking panel fronts.
Line with cotton fabric, andtop stitch decorative cuffs.
Personalize with embroidered names.

For place mats and table toppers:

Panel Quilting Mastery

Set each place with a different paneled design.
Bind and quilt layers together.
Adorn with themed ricrac, ribbon, or rickrack.

Spread seasonal cheer with holiday spirited panel quilting!

Idea Journals with Interchangeable Panels

Spark creativity by designing a fabric notebook or journal with mix and match quilted panel covers.

To make:

Quilt and bind fabric panels individually into book cover sizes.
Adorn covers with layered appliqué, embroidery, or mixed media.
Allow panel covers to overhang book base edges slightly.
Tack quilted covers to inside book covers lightly, to allow swapping out.
Customize your journal to suit each day's artistic mood and motivations!

Heirloom Memory and Photo Quilts

Create touching tributes and gifts preserving cherished memories, in fabric, by incorporating meaningful panels.

For memory quilts:

Print blocks of scanned memorabilia onto photo fabric sheets.
Fussy cut into panels and frame treasured pieces with care.
Add solid blocks embroidered with dates, quotes, or notes,

For photo quilts:

Print special photos directly onto printable cotton or silk.
Assemble photo squares into paneled layouts.
Enhance with subtle embroidery and embellishing.

Heartfelt photo and memory quilts become lasting sentimental keepsakes.

Upcycling Panel Scraps

Avoid wasting panel remnants by repurposing them into petite projects! Scraps transform into:

Jewelry, like fabric earrings, brooches, bracelets and necklaces
Embellished iron-on patches adorning jackets and hats
Coasters featuring fussy cut or funky upcycled motifs
Strips sewn into bias tape edging other projects

With a little creativity, nothing goes to waste. Fill your home with handmade panel treasures!

More Unique Projects Showcasing Quilt Panels

In addition to traditional quilts, creatively repurpose your beloved panels into these additional modern home, fashion, and unexpected items:

Framed Mini Art Quilts

Transform fussy cut panel sections into dazzling framed art pieces combining free motion stitching, appliqué, and embellishment in small, abstract compositions.

Quilted Magnet Board

Cover a magnetic board base with quilted fabric panels, adding whimsy with ribbon trims, layered appliqués, and exuberant quilting. Keep layers lightweight enough for magnet adhesion.

Mug Rugs

Whip up quilted and bound fabric "rugs" just right for protecting tables from morning mugs. Print or embroider clever sayings like "If the mug fits" onto panel tops.

Panel Quilting Mastery

Bulletin Boards

Transform an office or classroom bulletin board into a lively focal feature by wrapping it in a quilted and embellished fabric panel collage. Tack layers at top edges only with ribbon or trim.

Kindle or Tablet Covers

Customize e-reader covers by quilting front flaps with fabric panel designs suited to your reading tastes. Add storage pockets inside using contrast prints.

Key Fobs

Keep keys organized on handy quilted fabric panel key chains. Swivel lobster clasps attached at sides of quilted rectangles keep keys accessible but together.

Puzzle Covers

Preserve completed jigsaw puzzle masterpieces permanently, under glass, and framed in a quilted fabric panel matching the puzzle image, for personalized nostalgic wall art.

Quilted Table Runners

Protect tabletops from scratches and spills by machine or hand quilting scene setter fabric panels, with coordinating strip backing and batting. Bind the ends.

With a little creativity, beloved panels transform into amazing personalized pieces.

Creative Display Ideas for Showcasing Panels

Take panels beyond quilts and crafts by displaying them as artworks in innovative ways:

Textile Wall Panels

Carolyn Holt

Mount panels individually in floating frames or grouped in eclectic arrangements as artistic wall accents. Add LED backlighting for extra drama.

Fabric Wrapped Canvases

Stretch and staple panels over plain canvas stretcher bars for instant transformation into "paintings" ready to hang or prop on mantles or shelves.

Pillow Spotlighting

Incorporate panels into plush display pillows, propping open to showcase paneled faces when not in functional use. Ties or loops keep pillows neatly closed.

Quilted Room Dividers

Transform large graphic panels into freestanding, folding screens. While partitioning space and displaying stunning fabric art, viewers can see from both sides thanks to transparency.

Fabric Lampshades

Wrap lampshades in quilted or whole panels, matching room decor. Use lightweight fabric and minimal batting for proper lampshade construction.

Outdoor Banners

Weatherproof beloved panels into hanging banners anchored between posts, to define and decorate outdoor spaces using acrylic textile mediums to seal fabric.

Temporary Panels

Adhere quilted panel art, pouches, and pillows in guest rooms using damage-free, removable adhesive strips for quick customization between visitors.

Panel Quilting Mastery

With clever solutions, beloved panels come out of storage into the spotlight as artistic focal points, enhancing any space with vibrant spirit!

Carolyn Holt

Chapter 11
Gallery of Inspiring Panel Quilts

While quilting with panels follows core fundamentals, the variety of stunning outcomes is limited only by imagination. The boundless creativity of the global quilting community provides endless inspiration through shared panel quilting projects.

In this chapter we'll tour a curated gallery showcasing the amazing diversity of panel quilting techniques, layouts, themes and styles. Prepare to be amazed and inspired!

Traditional Floral Medallion Quilts

Nothing conveys timeless beauty like a medallion quilt starring a central floral panel.

Cherished Linens, by Jacquelynne Steves, highlights rich ruby and gold roses within Old World inspired blocks and exquisite hand quilting. A traditional treasure.

Medallion Perfection, by Rockin' Bobbin Quilting, frames brilliant burgundy botanicals within scalloped pieced borders and intricate feather curls. It's crafted with expert technical precision.

Antique Bouquet, by K. Anna Designs, presents romantic watercolor florals on linen within dynamic pieced sawtooth borders. The complementary palette pairing creates harmony.

Carolyn Holt

Sunflower Medallion, by The Calico Cat, seamlessly spotlights glowing golden blooms within nine-patch block squares. With lovely corner floral vignettes, you get sunny simplicity.

These medallions masterfully balance focal panels with supportive piecing to let botanical motifs shine as the stars.

Vintage Inspired Storytelling Quilts

Warmly nostalgic feedsack panels evoke simpler times on charming vignettes and storytelling quilts.

Cottage Garden Retreat, by Penny Layman, hand quilts whisper-thin appliquéd floral vignettes on cotton panels with delicate natural motifs.

Sunday Best, by Sherri K. Falls, altars clustered printed panels alongside meaningful memorabilia on flowing fields of vintage fabrics, delicately embellished. This artwork is full of touching traditions.

Hazel's Kitchen, by Quilt Fabrication, plays with pattern scale, pairing tiny gingham, buffalo check, fruit canning labels, and an oversized stove panel creatively. This quilt is full of rustic charm.

My Great Aunt's Flower Garden, by Laura Preston, borders panels capturing bygone lilies, birds, and butterflies in nostalgic framed settings with precise needle turn applique. It is certainly heirloom quality.

These impeccable quilts lovingly honor enduring stories and connections stitched into timeworn inspiring panels.

Modern Graphic Block Quilts

Geometry goes glam on bold modern quilts when printed panels repeat graphic tessellating blocks.

Pixel Play, by Violet Craft, fuses chunky pixelated blocks in vivid pops on deep gray with narrow neon green sashing for electrifying energy.

Looking Glass, by Violet Craft, again experiments by reflecting off-center kaleidoscopic motifs across meringue cream.

Panel Quilting Mastery

De Stijl Quilt, by Don't Call Me Betsy, marries Mondrian's signature style with three foot wide De Stijl fabric panels in a king quilt. It's balanced simplicity provides the purist joy.

Mad About Plaid, by A Quilting Life, transforms oversized buffalo plaid panels into a dynamic toddler blanket with prairie points adding the appearance of motion. This is a quilt full of youthful whimsy.

Repeating bold modern graphic panels creates punchy quilts brimming with spirited style.

Artistic Freeform Panels

Unleashing panels into original freeform shapes opens endless creative possibilities.

A Walk in the Woods, by Marla Varner, intuitively fuses sliced forest panel prints and rectangles with improvised curvature, painterly dyeing, and exquisite custom quilting. This piece is pure organic artistry.

Ode to Bees, by Marla Varner, buzzes with energetic asymmetry created from fragmented bee print panels, strip piecing, and heavy free motion quilting. It's laid out in a bold, daring composition.

Improv Pixel Play, by Quilttician, empowers large-scale pixels with non-linear arrangements, dynamic negative space, and dense texture quilting. Fearless freedom is represented in this art

Color Pool, by Aliza Keller, art journaled with dye on panels, creates atmospheric ombre gradients and ripples through water distortion. Vibrant, flowing expressionism is portrayed in this quilt.

By fracturing convention, quilters invent freely, with panels as their guide, to imaginative new means of storytelling.

Whimsical Novelty Panels

Charming and cheeky printed novelty panels create playful quilts full of personality.

Carolyn Holt

A Recipe for Comfort, by Holly DeGroot, savors retro kitchen panels amongst popping fruit and gingham prints. The juicy cherry border ties it together in delightful nostalgia.

School Days, by April Rosenthal, frames youthful alphabet, number, and shape panels alongside polka dot prints with school photo inserts. Timeless toddler delight is born here.

Hocus Pocus, by Corey Yoder, bewitches with pixelated potions, bubbling cauldrons, and aspens against black batiks. Vintage Halloween magic shines in this piece.

A Dog's Life, by Sherri K. Falls, commands canine cuteness overload with frolicking puppies and humorous dog sayings, on pint sized panels. Ruff ruff!

These hip and happy quilts prove panels can be playful when stitched together with a sense of humor and childlike joy.

Artisan Fiber Paintings

Master quilters elevate meticulously embellished pictorial and painted panels into exceptional fiber art.

Spring's Promise, by Charlotte Angotti, lovingly captures spring's fleeting beauty through delicately shaded and quilted thread, painting over silk panels. Painterly perfection is seen in her work.

Sea of Dreams by, Lisa Walton, sails to new horizons, immersing panels in turbulent waves, ethereal skyscapes, and glints of metallic golds. It's full of remarkable innovation.

My Secret Garden, by Patty Young, masterfully mixes a collage of her private garden sanctuary. It's bursting with dimensional florals, beads, buttons, and baubles over inky printed panels. Pure enchantment is found in this garden.

Panel Quilting Mastery

Fox in the Flower Garden, by Corey Yoder, mimics antique folk embroidery, hand quilting, and Trapunto textures to embellish her whimsical woodland portrait panel. Virtuosic handiwork sparkles here.

These visionary works exhibit the pinnacle of artistic expression achievable through panel quilting. Their remarkable techniques prompt imagination.

As these few samples demonstrate, quilters who embrace panels as their muse are only limited by their own creativity. All styles, skill levels, and tastes find inspiration. We hope this gallery spurs you in pursuing your own panel possibilities!

What will you create?

More Dazzling and Diverse Panel Quilting

The creativity of the quilting community never ceases to amaze and delight. Let's continue our virtual gallery tour with even more talent and diversity in quilting with panels:

Dimensional Sculptural Quilts

Some visionaries take quilting into three dimensions, sculpting fabric around forms.

Draped in History, by Carole Lyles Shaw, impressionistically molds historic African textile fragments over wire dress forms, for haunting shadowed dimension. Provocative artistry re-creates history.

Goddess of Africa, by Diana Bennett-Williams, similarly suspends bold graphic panels on goddess figures, weaving in beads, embroidery, and divine symbolism. It empowers invocation.

Origami Ring Quilt, by Geta Grama, stitches geometric panels into an intricate latticework of folded rings in motion. Hypnotic kinetic energy fills this artwork.

Carolyn Holt

All That Jazz, by Carol E. Anderson, improvises slicing and draping panels into an exuberant abstract portrait bust, heavily stitched and quaking with omnidirectional rhythm.

Sculptural shaping carries panels into exciting new frontiers of quilted art free from constraints.

Innovative Panel Inserts and Borders

Panels shine bright when scattered across pieced tops and integrated creatively into borders too.

Hexie Hilarity, by Happy Zombie, stitches a playful jigsaw of hundreds of close-set hexagons around colorful carved pumpkin panels for autumnal energy.

A Field of Sunflowers, by Pat Sloan, scatters cheery clustered sunflower sprays edge-to-edge over patchwork prairies, and drawssunny smiles.

Sewing Notions Border, by Love Bug Studios, imaginatively applied rickrack, buttons, and sewing notions trims project from sawtooth borders alongside retro sewing panels.

Summer Shadows, by Roseann Kermes, adorns pieced Dresden Plate borders with dimensional prairie points, concealing tiny floral panels. Tactile poetry.

With open minds, panels transform into amazing accents and artistic focus points.

Improvisational Abstracts

Splicing panels abstractly reveals newfound freedom.

Moon Over Water, by Carol E. Anderson, slices gradients asymmetrically across monochromatic panels, in a heavily stitched way, and wildly irregular.

Panel Quilting Mastery

Kandinsky Circles, by Aliza Keller, intuitively pieces round fussy cut motifs from graphic panels over fluid wavy backgrounds.

Lone Star, by Gwen Marston, liberats panels into luminous. off-kilter stars dancing across inky space. Daring asymmetry makes this quilt a masterpiece.

Crystal Nebulae, by Mel Beach, fractures panels into crystalline galaxies, embellishing with prism batiks, metallic shine, dense quilting, and embroidered nebulae. A cosmic vista shines through this art.

With a spirit of adventure, panels fuse into abstract poetry in motion.

Young and Lively Panels

Vibrant panels craft delighted heirlooms for little ones.

A is for Animals, by April Rosenthal, playfully parades a child's animal alphabet menagerie, neatly framed, and nicely saturated. Toddler approved joy abounds from this design!

Pond Life, by Carole Lyles Shaw, magnetically immerses panels of textured fish, turtles, and frogs into their natural quilt habitat of rippled blues. Tactile immersion and playfulness show up here.

Dynamic Dinosaurs, by Deb Strain, has time traveled Jurassic superstars into a playful lineup of spunky dinos appliquéd with toothy grins. Prehistoric pals make this fun!

Woodland Wanderer's Quilt, by Don't Call Me Betsy, enchants a little explorer's dreams with cozy flannel backed panels of magical moonlit forest creatures. Slumber time security and peacefulness glow from this quilt.

Showstopping Masterpiece Panel Quilting

Let's conclude our inspirational quilt gallery with jaw-dropping showstoppers representing the pinnacle of panel possibilities:

Carolyn Holt

Ultimate Medallion Mastery

Some medallion works represent the apex of the art form.

My Blue Heaven, by Linda Hahn, spotlights an effervescent 30-inch panel within a kaleidoscope of tinted tessellating rings, sawtooth borders, prairie points, and 22,000 hand quilted stitches. Virtuosic precision is definitely recognized here.

Spring Bouquet, by Sharon Schamber, frames ravishing violet florals within concentric rings of flawless seams, embroidered vines, and 240 hand quilted feathers. Meticulous mastery floats throughout her artwork.

Consummate technical skill elevates medallions' visual richness when precise workmanship matches the splendor of resplendent focal panels.

Mind BlowingLarge Scale Quilts

Supersized graphic panels hold their own, becoming entire quilt tops.

Double Rainbows, by Cherry Guidry and Jennifer Dick, dazzled with six foot wide rainbow ombre panels kaleidoscoped into vibrant rays.

Heaven's Bridge, by Sharon Schambers, billows nine yards of crimson and ivory between towering Roman columns ablaze with meticulous quilting. Breathtaking grandeur and style show up in this quilt.

Going big makes strong, graphic panels the star attraction, with artistic placement and framing details supporting their bold authority.

Dimensional Adept Artistry

Some visionaries attain the capacity to artistically develop dimension in quilts, through astounding technique.

Autumn's Last Stand, by Laura Wasilowski, dissolves natural fragments into painterly watercolor networks, swirled with embroidery. Passionate finesse weaves this design.

Panel Quilting Mastery

The Peaceable Kingdom, by Karen Stone, floods her panel menagerie with expressive brushwork, then intricately needles each creature in luminous detail. Awe-inspiring sensitivity brings this quilt to life

With devoted dedication, panels become vehicles for spirit made tactile. Their astonishing techniques expand panel possibilities.

We hope you feel empowered to begin your own panel quilting journey by the visionary examples in this chapter and throughout this guide. Mentors provide pathways, but only you can determine the creative destination. Our final advice is simply to trust your passion and skills, take risks, and enjoy the adventures ahead. Happy quilting!

145

Closing Remarks

As we reach the final pages of this comprehensive guide to quilting with panels, we hope you feel newly emboldened to pursue panel quilting and are brimming with inspiration on the artistic potential.

Throughout these chapters, we've explored every facet of working with printed quilt panels - from selecting the perfect designs to complement your style, skill level, and project vision; to preparing panels for flawless piecing and construction.Strategizing layouts and incorporating supportive settings to best showcase the panels was discussed, as well as quilting and finishing considerations. We've also shown how embellishment and multiple displays make panels shine.

A gallery tour shared the astounding diversity of panel possibilities, from straightforward beginner-friendly layouts, all the way to elaborate showstopping art quilts demonstrating the pinnacle of possibility. We aimed to spark beginners with accessible projects, while providing advanced quilters insights into fine-tuning technique and exploring more innovative applications.

Quilting offers a universal language - a means of storytelling, memorializing, documenting emotion, decoding meaning, and connecting us across cultures. Panels empower every quilter, allowing focus on technique while incorporating touches of ready-made artistry. Yet as conduits for expression, panels come most fully alive only when your vision ignites their possibilities.

We hope this guide illuminates those possibilities and equips you to manifest your own quilting dreams with panels. Trust your instincts, embrace the unknown, and enable panels to guide your spirit. Immerse fully in the process - from first inspirations to adding the final stitch. The beauty is in the doing.

Carolyn Holt

May your path ahead overflow with creativity, connection, discovery, and joy. Our final guidance is simply to begin. Turn intention into action. Select some beloved panels and fabrics, gather your tools, and start transforming fabric to art, stitch by stitch. The rest will flow out of love.

Now venture forth and share your unique gifts! We cannot wait to see the stunning quilts, stories, and meaning you will co-create.